Whereas ye know not what shall be on the morrow. For what is your life? It is even a vapour, that appeareth for a little time, and then vanisheth away.

—James 4:14 (KJV)

Sweet Carolina MYSTERIES

Roots and Wings
Picture-Perfect Mystery
Angels Watching Over Me
A Change of Art
Conscious Decisions
Surrounded by Mercy
Broken Bonds
Mercy's Healing
To Heal a Heart
A Cross to Bear
Merciful Secrecy
Sunken Hopes
Hair Today, Gone Tomorrow

Sweet Carolina
MYSTERIES

HAIR TODAY, GONE TOMORROW

Leslie Gould

Sweet Carolina Mysteries is a trademark of Guideposts.

Published by Guideposts Books & Inspirational Media
100 Reserve Road, Suite E200
Danbury, CT 06810
Guideposts.org

Copyright © 2023 by Guideposts. All rights reserved.

This book, or parts thereof, may not be reproduced, stored in a retrieval system, or transmitted in any form or by any means, electronic, mechanical, photocopying, recording, or otherwise, without the written permission of the publisher.

This is a work of fiction. While the setting of Mercy Hospital as presented in this series is fictional, the location of Charleston, South Carolina, actually exists, and some places and characters may be based on actual places and people whose identities have been used with permission or fictionalized to protect their privacy. Apart from the actual people, events, and locales that figure into the fiction narrative, all other names, characters, businesses, and events are the creation of the author's imagination and any resemblance to actual persons or events is coincidental.

Every attempt has been made to credit the sources of copyrighted material used in this book. If any such acknowledgment has been inadvertently omitted or miscredited, receipt of such information would be appreciated.

Scripture references are from the following sources: *The Holy Bible, King James Version* (KJV). *The Holy Bible, New International Version* (NIV). Copyright © 1973, 1978, 1984, 2011 by Biblica, Inc. Used by permission of Zondervan. All rights reserved worldwide. www.zondervan.com.

Cover and interior design by Müllerhaus
Cover illustration by Bob Kayganich at Illustration Online LLC.
Typeset by Aptara, Inc.

This book was previously published under the title *Hair Today, Gone Tomorrow* as part of the *Miracles & Mysteries of Mercy Hospital* series.

ISBN 978-1-959634-82-9 (hardcover)
ISBN 978-1-959634-84-3 (epub)
ISBN 978-1-959634-83-6 (epdf)

Printed and bound in the United States of America
10 9 8 7 6 5 4 3 2 1

HAIR TODAY, GONE TOMORROW

Chapter One

Joy Atkins spun the greeting card display stand around, noting the collection of Father's Day cards with a lump in her throat. The holiday was just over a week away.

Many customers who were shopping for a Get Well card in the last week chose a Father's Day card—or two—also. Several hospital staff had purchased them too, grateful for the convenience. Joy suspected she'd sell even more cards during the week ahead.

Father's Day was still a hard day for Joy, two years after her husband, Wilson, had passed. Thankfully her daughter, Sabrina, had her own husband to celebrate, with the help of their two daughters. But Joy knew it was difficult for all of them too. Wilson had been a wonderful father and grandfather, not to mention a fantastic husband.

She'd always hosted a barbecue back at their home in Texas, starting when Sabrina was six months old. Back then, Joy's father was one of the honored guests. Friends and neighbors attended too. Wilson manned the grill, cooking ribs and brats. After she was grown, Sabrina and her family would travel from Charleston to attend. It had been one of Joy's favorite days of the year.

She stepped away from the cards and resumed dusting the collection of vases. Life changed. Nothing remained the same. Here she was in Charleston now, blessed to be close to Sabrina's family.

Still, she missed Wilson every single day. And, honestly, every time someone bought a Father's Day card, she felt a pang of grief. She was going to change that. From now on, she'd pray for that family—and others too—that they'd be blessed as they celebrated.

A commotion in the lobby caught Joy's attention, and she stepped to the window, her duster still in hand. Sassie Crane, who wore a black blouse, a leopard print pencil skirt, and strappy sandals, was hurrying toward the lobby exit with a man following behind her. Joy stepped to the doorway of the gift shop. Sassie caught sight of her and veered toward her, dodging in front of an older couple and slipping inside the shop as the man kept going.

Joy stayed in the doorway for a minute, but the man didn't return. He had thick gray hair, was rather tall and lean, and wore a goatee. Joy didn't recognize him.

Joy turned back but didn't see Sassie at first. Finally she spotted her examining a blown glass vase, her long dark bangs from her asymmetrical haircut hanging over one eye.

"What was that all about?" Joy asked.

Sassie raised her head, flipped her bangs aside, and met Joy's gaze. "I'm not sure." Sassie laughed a little. "A case of mistaken identity, I'm guessing." She held up the seafoam-colored vase. "This is perfect for the addition to my spa—I'm going to have a big reopening in two weeks. The palette is sea cottage chic. Pastels and neutrals. I'll take it."

Not only was *chic* a good adjective for Sassie's decor in her expanded spa, but it was for Sassie too. Joy guessed, by the age of

Sassie's daughter, that Sassie was in her midfifties, but she could easily pass for forty.

As Joy rang up the vase, she debated whether to ask about Sassie's waiting list. Joy had been on it for over a month, hoping to have Sassie, who was the premier stylist in Charleston, cut her hair.

After she ran Sassie's card, she said, "Any chance you have an opening on your wait list?"

"That's right, you are on *that* list," Sassie said. "As a matter of fact, I had a cancellation this morning and haven't had a chance to fill it. If you'd like it, it's yours."

"What time?" Joy wrapped the vase in tissue paper.

"Three thirty today."

"Perfect," Joy said. "I'll be there." She had nothing else planned for her late Friday afternoon.

Sassie's daughter, Ashley, was friends with Sabrina. Joy had met Ashley when she first moved to Charleston, and then she'd been introduced to Sassie at a garden party a couple of months ago.

Of course, Joy had known of Sassie before then. She owned and operated Sassie's Salon and Spa, which was located kitty-corner from the hospital in the historic Crane Building. Joy sometimes got pedicures there with her friend Shirley and Shirley's mother, Regina, but she hadn't been able to get an appointment for a haircut.

Joy placed the vase in a bag.

"Thank you." Sassie gave Joy another smile as she took the purchase. "See you at three."

Perplexed, Joy said, "Three thirty? That's what you just said."

"Right." Sassie smiled again. "Three thirty. See you then."

Joy switched the sign to Closed at three.

As she stepped out the door, closed it, and then began to lock it, Evelyn Perry, the director of the hospital's records department called out, "Hello, Joy! Where are you off to this early?" Evelyn wore her silver hair in a bun on her head with a pencil tucked in it.

Joy often stuck around until three thirty or four, especially on a Friday, to tidy up for the weekend. Joy waved at her friend. "I finally got a hair appointment with Sassie."

Evelyn smiled. "I was just thinking about her."

"Any reason why?"

"I could swear I saw her cousin in the lobby this morning."

Joy tilted her head. "Which was unexpected, I'm guessing?"

Evelyn nodded. "On the other hand, perhaps it wasn't him at all. I haven't seen him in thirty years, which doesn't mean he hasn't been around, but the man I saw is how I imagine her cousin would look now."

"Gray hair and a goatee?"

Evelyn's eyebrows shot up. "How did you know?"

"I saw a man who looked like that following Sassie through the lobby this morning, right before she came into the shop."

Evelyn shrugged. "I'm probably imagining things." She gave Joy a wave. "Have fun getting your hair cut."

"Thanks! Have a wonderful weekend."

"You too." Evelyn smiled and continued on to the records department.

As Joy stepped out of the main entrance of the hospital, she took her cell phone from her purse and pressed Sabrina's number.

The call went straight to voice mail. Joy said hello and then, "Guess what? I'm on my way to Sassie's for a haircut. Talk to you soon!"

Joy held her phone in her hand as she waited for the crosswalk signal to change. Once it did, as she crossed the street, her phone buzzed. A text from Sabrina. Great! Have fun! Maybe I'll see you later—I'm going to have dinner with Ashley while Rob takes the girls to play tennis. Eloise keeps saying she wants to learn. It's cool enough that I think I'll ride my bike.

Joy "loved" the text and then slipped her phone back into her purse. Rob had given Sabrina a bicycle for Mother's Day, and she'd been riding whenever she could, with the girls and by herself, often with their dog Mopsy on a leash and running along beside her in their neighborhood. But sometimes she went on a long solo bike ride just for fun.

Ahead of her was the entrance to Sassie's Salon and Spa. The two-story Crane Building took up a small, odd-sized block. The second floor was all apartments. The front side, which faced the bay, was a line of shops, including Sassie's. The back was a warehouse. Sassie was remodeling half the space to expand her spa. Joy guessed, with the demand for retail space in the downtown area, that the rest of the warehouse would soon be repurposed too and rented out. Sassie had an amazing resource in the building along with an admirable business that she'd built since she was a young woman.

Joy continued on, pushing through the front door. The interior of the shop was decorated in what seemed to already be a sea cottage chic theme. The walls were a seafoam green while the accents were tan, teal, and rose. A sea salt candle burned on the counter, filling the shop with the scent of the sun on warm waves.

Ashley stood at the check-in. She had her mother's dark hair, although she wore it long and straight. "Joy," she said. "How nice to see you. What can I do for you?"

"I have a three thirty appointment with your mom."

Ashley glanced down at the book in front of her.

"She told me she had a cancellation. I was on the wait list."

"Oh. I don't remember Hannah ever canceling before." Ashley glanced up and smiled. "It's your lucky day."

Joy smiled back. "I agree."

"Take a seat," Ashley said. "She'll be ready in a few minutes."

"I'm early," Joy said.

"You'll have time for a cup of tea. Or a glass of water."

"I'll take the water."

Ashley stepped to a beverage bar off to the side and filled a glass, pouring from a pitcher of ice water and sliced limes. Joy took the drink, settled in a pale pink leather chair next to a tabletop water fountain, and leaned her head against the back of the chair. She could hear the buzz of a power tool. She glanced at Ashley.

"We're turning the first floor of the warehouse into our expanded spa," Ashley explained.

"Oh right," Joy said. "Your mother mentioned that this morning."

"We'll have a grand reopening in two weeks."

"Sounds lovely."

After a moment of silence, Ashley said, "I'm having dinner with Sabrina tonight."

"That's what she told me," Joy said. "It's a rare night off for her."

"Seriously," Ashley said. "I've been wanting to get together with her forever."

"She's wanting that too."

Ashley's husband, Barry, had died six months before in a freak sailing accident. Sabrina, along with her best friend, Amanda, had been there for Ashley as much as they could after the tragedy.

"Is Amanda joining you?"

Ashley shook her head. "She's working a long shift today." Amanda was a doctor at Mercy.

A couple of minutes later, Sassie appeared in the doorway and said, "Come on back, Joy," just as a tall woman with beautiful auburn hair came striding through the front door.

"Hannah," Ashley said and then spun toward her mother.

"Hannah," Sassie echoed. "You canceled your appointment."

The woman shrugged. "I changed my mind."

A few minutes later, Joy sat in one salon chair in Sassie's studio while Hannah sat next to her. The other two chairs were filled with the clients of two additional stylists. Everyone but Joy was talking. She sat silently, listening.

Sassie stood behind Hannah's chair. "I'll get Joy started first with her color and then begin yours."

Hannah wrinkled her nose.

Sassie patted the woman on the shoulder. "You can't cancel your appointment and expect me not to fill it."

"But it's been my appointment for the last thirty years."

"Thirty-seven," Sassie retorted. "No, thirty-eight."

Hannah sighed. "Who's counting?"

Both Sassie and Hannah looked amazing. Joy couldn't believe they were in their midfifties.

Hannah lowered her voice. "Parker was acting strange this morning. That's why I canceled. I was hoping to get him a doctor's appointment."

"How is he this afternoon?"

"Better."

"Maybe it's his new medication."

"Maybe…" Hannah took a sip from the metal bottle she held in her hand. "I want to talk with the doctor about that. We have an appointment for Wednesday."

Sassie patted Hannah's shoulder again. "Did you bring a book?"

Hannah smiled and reached in her big handbag that was still in her lap. "I did."

"Good girl," Sassie said. "I'll be with you in no time."

"You could go ahead and do Hannah's color first," Joy said, feeling as if she'd stolen Hannah's appointment.

Hannah shook her head. "No. Sassie is right. I canceled."

"But I'm not in a hurry," Joy said. "I'm happy to wait."

Hannah pursed her lips. "I do need to pick up Lindsay at five thirty."

"Are you sure, Joy?" Sassie asked.

"Positive." Joy reached for her bag and pulled *Growing Peonies in the South* from it. "I brought a book too."

"Bless your heart." Sassie turned her attention to Hannah, although she continued speaking to Joy.

"I've been doing Hannah's hair since I graduated from beauty school." Sassie paused a moment. "Actually, since high school. She used to let me experiment on her. God bless her soul for all of eternity for trusting me the way she did."

Hannah grinned. "Remember the Farrah Fawcett hairdo you gave me? Every single hair was layered. And dyed blond."

Sassie laughed. "Sophomore year. Parker took one look at you and asked you to the prom, even though he was a senior."

"And I turned him down to go with Ernest." There was a long, awkward pause, and then Hannah said, "A week later you dyed my hair auburn." Hannah touched the ends of her hair as Sassie mixed the hair dye.

"And Parker loved that too," Sassie said.

"Ha." Hannah shook her head. "Not as much as I have. We really were the Dream Team."

Sassie laughed again. "Never forget that we started out as the *Dare to* Dream Team back in middle school."

"That was when it was just you and me, before we let the boys join. We were so desperate to make something of ourselves."

"And we have." Sassie met her friend's eyes in the mirror.

Hannah smiled in agreement.

Joy opened her book and began reading, half listening to Sassie and Hannah's conversation. Lindsay was Hannah and Parker's daughter. It sounded as if she was in high school. There was no mention of any other children.

"Do you remember Lindsay's nanny—Rochelle?"

Sassie murmured, "Yes, of course."

"She moved back to town. She has a baby of her own and asked Lindsay to babysit."

"How sweet."

"Except Lindsay has absolutely no time for that—" Hannah paused. "Nor the need. I was surprised Rochelle would even ask."

Joy glanced up from her book and snuck a quick look at Sassie. She seemed to be concentrating intensely on Hannah's hair. She was literally biting her lip. Perhaps she was simply concentrating on not responding.

Positioning her book closer to her face, Joy reread the first paragraph and then kept reading. The more she read—that peonies could do well in the South, including South Carolina, but needed well-drained soil and lots of space—the less she was aware of the conversation going on next to her.

When Sassie stepped behind her, Joy was surprised she was done with applying the color to Hannah's hair already. Joy glanced to her left. Hannah sat with her head slathered in dye, now reading her own book.

Sassie lifted a section of Joy's hair. "What do you have in mind?"

"The same color plus a good trim but with more texture."

"How about a shade lighter on the color? I think that will work with your skin tone, plus with summer starting it will give you a lift."

Joy hesitated.

"Believe me." Hannah looked up from her book. "Trust Sassie when it comes to your hair. And pretty much everything else too."

"Yes, trust me with your hair, but I don't know about *everything* else." Sassie slipped on a new pair of gloves. "I'm sure Joy has everything else figured out by now."

Joy smiled. "I'm sure no one has *everything* figured out, no matter how"—she cleared her throat—"*mature* they are."

Sassie laughed. "I wasn't implying that. You seem calm and collected is what I was getting at. Unlike some of us."

Joy couldn't imagine what Sassie was talking about. In every interaction she'd had with Sassie, she'd seemed more than calm and collected. She was a dignified woman who carried herself with confidence and grace and presented herself with a signature style. Even when being pursued through the lobby of the hospital that morning.

Instead of risking saying the wrong thing, Joy simply said, "A shade lighter sounds like fun." She watched in the mirror as Sassie mixed her color and then began applying it to her hair.

One of the stylists at the end of the row of chairs finished her client's hair and said, "They're ready for you in the spa."

"Great." The woman wiggled her toes. "I'm definitely ready for my pedicure."

The stylist walked the woman through the far door and then returned. "See you tomorrow," she said to Sassie.

"See you then." Sassie glanced up from Joy's hair. "Thank you for your good work."

After the stylist exited to the lobby, Joy could hear her speaking with Ashley. In a low voice, Sassie said to Joy, "Your Sabrina has been such a good friend to my daughter. She's really helped her the last few months."

Empathy flooded Joy. "I can't imagine going through everything Ashley has at such a young age."

"I know," Sassie said. "But still, you've been there. You know what Ashley's faced since Barry's passing, which is probably part of the reason Sabrina has been so understanding."

Joy hadn't thought of that connection, but it made sense. Sabrina had been a big support, even in her own grief, when Wilson passed away.

A thud startled Joy. Hannah's book had hit the floor. Sassie put the dye on the counter and bent to pick it up. As she stood, she asked, "Hannah, are you all right?"

Hannah's head jerked. "I must have dozed off." She took the book from Sassie and then reached for her water bottle, which she'd placed on the counter. She took a drink and then went back to her reading.

Sassie resumed spreading the dye on Joy's hair.

"How long have you had your salon?" Joy asked.

"I opened it up the day after I passed my state boards. I was nineteen years old."

"That's amazing."

"I didn't do it on my own," Sassie said. "My grandfather owned the building and gave me a big break on my lease. And a beautician who owned a salon in town gave me a deal on her equipment because she was retiring. I've had my challenges over the years, but for the most part, it's been a great run."

"No plans to retire?"

"Absolutely not," Sassie said. "Now that Ashley is working with me, I'm ready to go another twenty years at least."

Joy nodded. Sabrina had mentioned that Ashley was working with Sassie.

"With the upcoming expansion, I figure the best is yet to come," Sassie said. She finished spreading the dye over Joy's short hair. As Sassie turned to the sink, another thud, this time louder, startled Joy, and she jumped.

Hannah's metal bottle had hit the floor, followed by Hannah sliding out of the chair, her book falling out of her hand and smacking the tile too. Followed by the back of Hannah's head.

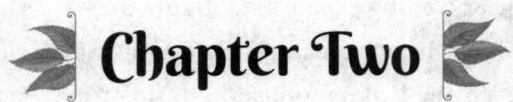

Chapter Two

SASSIE APPEARED TO BE PARALYZED, so Joy stepped down from her chair, bent in front of Hannah, and grabbed her wrist, feeling for a pulse. "Hannah," Joy said, "can you hear me?" The woman didn't stir.

Joy glanced up at Sassie, who stood with the hair dye in one hand and the applicator in the other. "Call 911."

Sassie didn't move.

"Do you need me to do it?"

Sassie nodded.

"Ashley," the remaining stylist shouted. "Call 911. Hannah fainted."

Ashley hurried in from the lobby, a cordless phone in her hand. "What happened?"

"Hannah's unconscious," Joy said, her fingers on Hannah's wrist. "She has a pulse, but I can't get her to wake—"

Before Joy ended her sentence, Ashley placed the call. "We need an ambulance at Sassie's Salon and Spa." She rattled off the address. "Hannah Hollingsworth fainted and is unresponsive. She has a pulse. She may have hit her head as she fell."

Joy said, "She definitely hit her head."

"Correction," Ashley said. "She did hit her head."

"Should I rinse her hair?" Sassie sputtered.

"I'll ask," Ashley said. She relayed the question over the phone and then shook her head at Sassie. Then, as she held her hand over the receiver, she said, "Don't move her. She may have a head or neck injury."

Sassie took a step away from Hannah. "Do you think she's unconscious because of the fall?"

"I don't know," Joy answered.

Hannah stirred a little.

"I'll tell the EMTs to have someone rinse her hair once they get her to the emergency room," Sassie said.

"Good idea, Mother," Ashley said.

The other stylist finished with her client and quickly escorted her to the lobby, saying to Ashley, "I'll run her card."

Ashley said, "Thank you. I hear a siren." She hurried into the lobby, still on the line.

Joy listened. She heard it too. Relieved, she stood, still staring at Hannah. The woman's eyelids were lined with blue veins. Underneath, her eyes fluttered. One leg was tucked underneath her, and her book was off to the side. Joy read the title. *Creating a Backyard Oasis*. It appeared Hannah liked to garden too—or more likely she came up with the ideas and hired others to do the work.

She left the book on the floor, not wanting to interfere with anything.

Ashley led the EMTs into the salon, and Joy stepped back to the far corner of the room while Sassie remained by the counter. Ashley answered all of their questions, not adding that she hadn't been in the room. However, she managed to relay the information correctly as they took Hannah's vitals and then placed a support collar around her neck and rolled her onto a backboard.

As the EMTs lifted Hannah onto the gurney, she opened her eyes. "What happened?"

"You seem to have fainted, ma'am," the older EMT said.

"Sassie?" Hannah tried to turn her head.

"Ma'am, please don't move."

For the first time since Hannah fell, Sassie budged from the spot where she'd been frozen. "I'm here." She stepped to Hannah's side, still holding Joy's hair dye in her hand.

"Where are they taking me?" Hannah asked.

"To the hospital."

"Come with me."

"I'll meet you there," Sassie said.

Tears filled Hannah's eyes.

Sassie stepped closer to the gurney. "You're going to be okay."

Hannah tried to smile, but instead tears flowed from her eyes and down the sides of her face.

Once the EMTs had Hannah out of the salon, Sassie looked at Ashley. "Darlin,' what do I do?"

"Call Parker and tell him what happened."

"Would you?"

Ashley took her cell phone out of the pocket of her seafoam green smock. She left a voice mail and then ended the call.

"Should I finish Joy's hair now?" Sassie asked Ashley.

"No," Joy answered. "Absolutely not. Go on to the hospital. I can rinse my own hair."

"I can do it," Ashley said. "And then, Mother, can you cut it next week?"

"Sure," Sassie said. "I can fit you in Monday at six thirty."

"Six thirty P.M.?" Joy clarified.

Sassie shook her head. "I have a seven thirty A.M. appointment. An hour earlier won't be a problem."

"All right." Joy got up early—she could make it work.

"Are you all right, Mother?" Ashley asked Sassie. "Do you want to wait and have me walk to the hospital with you?"

Sassie shook her head. "I told Hannah I'd be there. And I don't want you to cancel your time with Sabrina. I just have a couple of things to finish in my office, and then I'll go over to the emergency room." She left through the door to the spa.

It didn't take long for Ashley to rinse Joy's hair and then blow it dry. Sassie was right. The lighter color looked great—not only was it summery, but it also complemented Joy's skin tone.

When she took out her wallet to pay, Ashley said, "Pay on Monday after your haircut, after you're satisfied with everything."

"Okay," Joy said.

As she headed to the door, a man opened it. He was middle aged, completely bald, and clean shaven. He wore a purple polo shirt with a gold Sun Beauty emblem. He stepped inside. Ignoring Joy, he asked Ashley, "Is Sassie available?"

Ashley shook her head.

"I'm the new rep with Sun Beauty Supply and wanted to introduce myself. Is she in her office?"

Ashley shook her head again. "You'll need to come back on Monday."

The man smiled and stepped back out of the salon. He looked familiar to Joy, but she couldn't place where she'd seen him before. Perhaps he'd come into the gift shop at one time or another.

She gave Ashley a final goodbye and then left the salon. The man was nowhere to be seen.

Joy walked around the rear of the Crane Building, planning to turn on South Wharf Street, toward the waterfront, wanting a few minutes of calm after the excitement of the day before she walked home. In the distance the late afternoon sun hung low in the sky, sending light shimmering across the bay.

The squealing of a vehicle stopped Joy. She whirled around as a black SUV tore away from the curb alongside the Crane Building. She took a step back on the sidewalk, worried the car might jump the curb. She squinted as the car sped by her, but the windows were all tinted, and she couldn't see inside.

Someone screamed behind her, and Joy spun around. Sassie was running toward her. "Stop that vehicle!"

Joy knew she couldn't stop it, but she looked back at the vehicle, taking out her phone to at least get a picture of the license plate. The light at Bay Street was red. The SUV had to stop.

Or not.

It kept on going, turning into the intersection. Joy gasped, expecting a collision, anticipating the crunch of metal on metal. Instead the SUV hit a bicycle. Joy screamed as the bicyclist, a woman, flew up on the hood of the SUV. She screamed a second time when she realized the bicyclist with the neon yellow helmet was Sabrina.

Joy began to run. Sabrina rolled off the SUV onto the asphalt, to the side of the SUV. The driver ran over the bicycle and kept on going, turning left onto Wharf and disappearing. A group of people quickly gathered around Sabrina.

When Joy reached her, she elbowed her way through the group and knelt beside Sabrina. "Sabrina. Baby." She kept saying her name, waiting, hoping, praying for a response.

Sabrina's helmet was skewed to the side, and it was a full thirty seconds before she opened her eyes. "Mom?" She sounded disoriented. "What are you doing here?"

"I was just leaving Sassie's."

Sabrina rolled to her side, showing road rash on her arm and a scrape on her ankle that was bleeding.

Joy put her hand on Sabrina's shoulder. "Don't move."

"I'm okay."

Joy shook her head. "You need to stay still."

"Ma'am, she lost consciousness," a young man said, holding his phone close to his ear.

Joy made eye contact with him. "Are you calling 911?"

The man nodded. "I just gave the dispatcher the details. I'm still on the line."

"Did anyone get the license number of the vehicle?" Joy asked.

"There wasn't a plate on the front," a woman said. "And I was too stunned to see what was on the back as it sped away."

Sabrina said, "I'm fine, Mom. My helmet did what it was supposed to do."

"There's a big crack in your helmet," the woman said. "I wouldn't be so sure. I had a cousin—"

Sassie called out, "Joy! What happened!"

"That SUV you were trying to stop hit Sabrina."

Sassie's face fell for a moment, but then she knelt next to Joy and turned her attention to Sabrina. "How are you, darlin'?"

"Fine, but Mom won't let me get up."

"She's right. You need to stay still." Sassie looked at Joy. "Did someone call for an ambulance?"

"Yes." Joy gestured to the young man. "He did."

"How about the police?"

The young man stepped forward. "The dispatcher was going to send both, since it's a hit-and-run." He addressed the group. "We should stick around and give statements."

A car to the left honked its horn.

The young man waved at it and yelled, "Hold on. A bicyclist has been hit."

"Thank you," Joy said to the young man.

"You bet," he answered. "My name is Lance. I work at the hospital."

Joy glanced up at him. He appeared to be in his early twenties. Short hair. Bright dark eyes. She didn't recognize him. "So do I," she said. "In the gift shop."

"I just started in transportation," he said.

That would explain why she hadn't seen him.

Sassie pulled out her phone and sent a text. Immediately her phone beeped. "Ashley's on her way," she said.

Joy continued to kneel beside her daughter. "I need to call Rob."

Sabrina groaned. "Wait until I'm in the ER, okay? He has the girls with him. I'd scare them if they came now."

Joy pursed her lips.

Ashley arrived, out of breath. Sassie quickly told her what happened. Ashley, her phone already in her hand, placed a phone call. Joy could hear her sharp words. "You need to come now. There's been a hit-and-run, by an SUV connected to a crime at Sassie's Salon and Spa. Not only are there two crime victims, there's also a traffic jam of irate Friday drivers."

Ashley ended the call. "Who did this?"

"The driver of the SUV who was poking around my warehouse. He ran off when he saw me, and I didn't get a good look at him. He took an antique safe that belonged to my grandfather."

Ashley frowned. "I thought you were at the hospital."

"I was on my way—through the warehouse. I wanted to speak with the contractor, but he'd already left. I heard someone at the front door—I thought it was the contractor. But when I got there the safe was missing and the black SUV was pulling away from the curb."

For the second time that afternoon, an emergency siren wailed in the vicinity of the Crane Building.

"We'll talk about all of that later," Sassie said. "What matters now is Sabrina's health."

The siren grew closer. Joy wasn't surprised that it was a police car, most likely summoned by Ashley, that arrived first, before the ambulance.

The ambulance followed and although one of the officers, who seemed to know Ashley, questioned the witnesses, Joy didn't hear their answers. The other officer directed traffic around the ambulance and Sabrina.

The EMTs loaded Sabrina into the back of the ambulance. One commented on how well she'd withstood being hit by the SUV, but Joy knew she might have internal injuries.

"I'll meet you in the ER," Joy called out to Sabrina as she started to lift the mangled bike from the asphalt.

The police officer stopped her. "Leave it," he said. "We'll take it to the station as evidence."

"All right." Joy stepped to the sidewalk, eager to get to the hospital. Lance waved at her, and she waved back. She passed one of the police officers questioning Sassie.

"The only thing I've noticed so far that's missing is an antique safe. It was hidden behind a false wall the construction crew tore down a few days ago. I had them move it by the front door."

"Do you have security video?"

Sassie shook her head. "I'm in the middle of a remodel. The system has been down for a few days."

Joy felt sick to her stomach. She wanted whoever was responsible for hitting Sabrina caught.

"What was in the safe?" Joy asked.

"I don't know," Sassie answered. "I can't find the key. I contacted a locksmith but haven't heard back from him yet."

Ashley followed Joy. "I'll go to the hospital with you."

"Thank you." Joy was beginning to feel shaky. Sabrina could have been killed. But she couldn't let her mind go there. Sabrina was fine. She just needed to be checked out by an ER doc.

Joy needed to stay strong.

Sassie waved at Ashley and Joy. "I need to go back with the officer and show them where the safe was in the warehouse. Tell Hannah I'll get to the hospital as soon as I can."

"All right," Ashley called out. "See you soon." Then she said to Joy, "Mother's been acting strange all day."

"Well, a lot of strange things have happened."

"That's true," Ashley said. "I just don't know why she didn't go to the hospital right away, especially when Hannah asked her to."

Joy wondered too, but she didn't know Sassie well enough to speculate.

When they reached the hospital, as they stepped into the lobby, Anne came hurrying toward Joy and Ashley, her eight-year-old granddaughter, Addie, with her. Anne was a volunteer extraordinaire at the hospital and her husband, Ralph, was a chaplain. Joy stopped under the chandelier, whose cut-crystal pieces danced, sending spirals of tiny rainbows over the white marble floor.

They all said hello and then Ashley said, "I'll go check on Hannah."

"Has something happened?" Anne asked.

Joy felt a lump in her throat. "Sabrina was in an accident and is in the ER. She's conscious and doesn't seem to have broken anything but needs to get checked out."

"Oh, Joy," Anne said. "I'll stay with you."

Tears sprang into Joy's eyes. "Thank you. I appreciate that. But you have Addie to take care of, and I'll most likely just be here until Rob arrives with the girls."

Anne reached for Joy's hand and squeezed it. "Call if you need me to come back."

"I will."

"Did Sabrina tell you that Addie is signed up for the same sports camp as Eloise and Mallory, starting on Monday?"

"No," Joy answered.

"I can pick up your two girls after camp and keep them until Rob can come get them. I'm guessing Sabrina will be out of the hospital, but she might need extra rest."

"Thank you," Joy said. "I'll tell her."

Joy smiled at Addie and gave her a pat on the shoulder. Joy waved at Anne and then headed to the emergency room.

As she neared the emergency room, she heard a raised voice. A man's. She rounded the corner and saw Ashley, her arms crossed. Joy couldn't see the man's face—his back was turned to her. He wore navy pants and a light blue dress shirt. His voice was deep and loud. "Your mother poisoned Hannah."

"Parker," Ashley said, "don't be ridiculous."

"It's clear as day," the man shouted. "Attempted murder." He held out his cell phone. "I've already called the police. They're on their way."

Chapter Three

BY THE TIME JOY REACHED Ashley, the man had stormed off, back into the emergency room.

Ashley glanced up from her phone. "Did you hear that?"

Joy nodded. "I'm guessing that's Hannah's husband?"

"I just texted Mother to warn her, but she hasn't texted me back," Ashley said.

"She's probably still talking with the officer," Joy said. "Besides, he was being completely unreasonable. Hannah was probably dehydrated or overheated."

Ashley looked up from her phone again. "Hopefully she'll be here soon. She's been acting weird all day, but I know she wouldn't poison Hannah."

Joy couldn't imagine Sassie poisoning Hannah either. "Parker is upset. Maybe he's just blowing off steam." She felt anxious to get to Sabrina but asked, "How is Hannah doing?"

"I'm not sure," Ashley said. "I wish Mother would've come to the hospital when she said she was going to. None of this looks good."

Joy understood that, but the main concern had to be for Hannah's health—not how things looked.

"Have you seen Sabrina?" Joy asked.

"They just took her back," Ashley answered. "I was headed to see Hannah until Parker lit into me. I hurried out here with him so he wouldn't upset the entire emergency room." Ashley's phone beeped. She looked at it and then said, "Mother's on her way."

"All right," Joy answered. "I'm going on back to see Sabrina."

After she checked in at the desk, she walked to room three. Across the hall, Parker was still speaking loudly. "Sassie has done it this time. I'm going to call our lawyer about suing her."

"She didn't do anything," Hannah said. "You need to stop talking or leave. You're not helping."

Joy slipped in to see Sabrina.

"What's going on out there?" Sabrina asked.

"I'm not sure…." Joy smiled at her daughter. "How are you?"

"The same as when you saw me ten minutes ago. Fine. I have a headache is all. I want to go home."

"Let's see what the doctor says."

Sabrina groaned. "Did you call Rob?"

"Not yet," Joy answered.

A nurse Joy didn't recognize stepped into the room. "I need to take your vitals."

"Go call Rob, please," Sabrina said to Joy.

"Okay. I'll be right back." She headed out to the far corner of the waiting room. She'd made hard calls in her life before, the worst one being when she called Sabrina to tell her that her father was in the hospital after collapsing.

This wasn't one of those calls. Sabrina was alive. Still, Joy felt shaky at the near miss. Sabrina could have easily been killed.

She stared at her phone for a moment, inhaled deeply and then let her breath out slowly, and placed the call.

Rob answered with his usual cheerful, "Hello, Mom! What's up?"

Joy concentrated on keeping her voice calm. "Sabrina's okay, but she was riding her bike and an SUV hit her in the intersection of Bay and Wharf Streets. She's here at Mercy now."

"What?"

"I'm in the waiting room of the ER. I'll let you know as soon as we speak to the doctor."

"Are you sure she's okay?"

"She's conscious," Joy said. "Moving everything. She was ready to get up and walk away from the scene."

"Did she lose consciousness?"

"According to a witness, yes."

"I'm on my way." Rob yelled, "Girls! We need to go!"

"I'll take the girls once you get here," Joy said.

Rob didn't respond to Joy's statement. "See you ASAP," he said. The call ended as he yelled, "Come on!"

A few minutes later, as Joy told Sabrina about her call with Rob, Amanda slipped into the room. She wore a white lab coat over a navy blue blouse and black slacks, and her strawberry blond hair was piled on her head. "Sabrina, what in the world happened? I just saw Ashley out in the lobby."

"I'm fine, really," Sabrina said. "I mean"—she rolled her eyes—"I did get hit by a car, but miraculously I'm okay." She gestured to Joy. "But Mom wants to make sure."

"Of course," Amanda said. "You could have a head injury or internal injuries. You have to get checked out."

Sabrina sighed. "All right. If both my best friend and my mother insist—"

"And your doctor." Dr. Chad Barnhardt stood in the doorway with Shirley Bashore behind him, who piped up with, "And your ER nurse. I insisted that you be my patient."

Joy couldn't help but smile. Dr. Barnhardt and Shirley were both superheroes. Sabrina was in the best of hands.

Shirley stepped to the bed, putting her arm around Joy as she did. "Sabrina, how are you feeling?"

"Fine, I think," Sabrina said.

Dr. Barnhardt gave Joy a questioning look.

"Sabrina is my daughter," she explained.

"Ah." He turned to Sabrina. "Tell us what happened."

Sabrina gave a brief account of riding into the intersection of Bay and Wharf Streets and being hit by an SUV. "At least that's what I was told happened," she said. "I rolled up on the hood and then off, and landed on the pavement. My helmet is cracked. I woke up with Mom staring down at me."

Shirley winced.

"Any pain?" Dr. Barnhardt asked.

"I have a headache." Sabrina tapped the left side of her head.

"Blurred vision?"

"No."

"Other pain?"

"My arm. And ankle. Plus my side."

"All right." Dr. Barnhardt took out his penlight and began looking into Sabrina's eyes. "On the one hand, you're doing better than a lot of people who get hit by a vehicle. When I heard about the hit-and-run, I was expecting much worse. On the other hand, there are a lot of things we need to rule out."

Sabrina sighed. "Such as a head injury? Internal injuries?"

Dr. Barnhardt smiled. "Exactly."

"Am I going home tonight?" Sabrina asked.

"Possibly," he answered. "It all depends on what we find. We'll do a CT scan first."

Ten minutes later, Joy's phone rang. It was Rob, calling from the waiting room. "I'll be right out," she said.

She told Sabrina she was switching places with Rob.

"Tell Eloise and Mallory I'm fine," Sabrina said. "And then take them back home. I don't want them waiting here."

"I will," Joy said. "We'll get some dinner on the way."

When Joy left Sabrina's room, everything was quiet across the hall in Hannah's room. Joy guessed Parker had left.

When she reached the waiting room, the girls were sitting in chairs while Rob paced back and forth in front of them. On the far side, Parker stared at Sassie and Ashley, his arms crossed again. It was the first time she'd gotten a good look at him. He was tall and in good shape, with muscular arms. His hair was still dark although silver at the temples. He was a handsome man despite his demanding tone.

Finally, Sassie said, "You can't be serious, Parker. You know I'd never harm Hannah. She's my best friend. I adore both of you, along with Lindsay. I'd never hurt any of you. It would be like harming Ashley."

"I don't believe you," Parker said. "You're trying to stop me from buying your building."

"My building's not for sale. I'm expanding my business, remember? I have a reopening planned in two weeks. Why would I take on a remodel if I planned to sell the building?"

"You've done everything you can to block me."

Sassie stood. "The Crane Building is not for sale, and it never has been."

Parker crossed his arms and shouted, "You can't stop me by poisoning my wife. I'll sue."

"Be quiet," Sassie said. "Or I'm going to press charges against you for defamation."

"No one will care." Parker stalked away.

Sassie transferred her gaze to Joy. She gave her a wary smile. In return, Joy gave her a wave and then said hello to Rob.

"How is Sabrina doing?" Rob asked.

"The same," Joy answered. "She should have her CT scan soon. I'll get the girls some dinner and then take them home."

"Thanks." Rob started toward the hall.

"Room three," Joy said. "But check in at the desk first."

Rob stopped, hurried back to Mallory, and gave her a hug, and then he hugged Eloise. "Mimi will take you two home after you get some dinner. I'll see you there."

Six-year-old Mallory, who wore a purple top and a pink tutu, grabbed Joy's leg. Joy pulled her youngest granddaughter even closer.

Ten-year-old Eloise stood stoically a few feet away.

"Mommy's fine," Rob said, looking from Mallory to Eloise. "I'll call Mimi as soon as we know anything. If Mommy doesn't get to go home tonight, we'll come see her tomorrow." He stepped back and blew kisses to each of them. "Have fun at dinner."

"We will," Eloise said.

"Tell Mommy to get well soon," Mallory called out.

Rob waved and then turned back to the desk.

Eloise took a step closer to Joy. "I like the color of your hair, Mimi."

"Thank you." Joy had forgotten about the new color. She reached for Eloise and pulled her close for a side hug.

Ashley approached. "Do you want me to take the girls out for dinner?"

"Oh, that's kind of you," Joy said.

"Could Ashley come with us?" Eloise asked.

Joy glanced at Mallory. She was smiling and nodding her head.

"That's a great idea," Joy said. "Where shall we go?"

Sassie stood a few feet away, texting on her phone.

"Would you like to come with us?" Joy asked.

Sassie raised her head, a confused expression on her face.

"We're going out to dinner," Ashley said. "Do you want to come along?"

Sassie shook her head. "I need to go back to the shop and finish closing."

"I can do that," Ashley said. "After dinner."

Sassie shook her head again. "I'll do it and go on home." She yawned. "It's been quite the day."

"Are you going to check in with Hannah?"

Sassie frowned. "I don't think that's a good idea—not with Parker hovering around her and only leaving to rant at me."

"Mother." Ashley's voice was an annoyed whisper. "If you don't go see Hannah, it's going to look bad. Parker is accusing you, loudly, of poisoning Hannah. If you don't talk with Hannah, especially after you told her you'd meet her here, you're going to look suspicious."

"Don't be ridiculous." Sassie held up her phone. "I texted Hannah. She said Parker is being absurd. She doesn't want me to go back and see her."

Ashley rolled her eyes, clearly annoyed with her mother. "All right. But go on home. I'll close up the shop."

"Thank you," Sassie said. "I'll be in tomorrow morning."

"I thought you were going to start taking Saturdays off."

Sassie shrugged. "I have appointments. I'll be there."

"See you then."

Joy, Ashley, and the girls followed Sassie out of the waiting room. Joy expected Sassie to turn to the right and exit the hospital. Instead she went to the left. As Ashley and the girls kept going toward the exit, Joy slowed. Sassie stopped at the elevators. She wasn't going home. At least not yet. She was going to one of the other floors of the hospital.

"How about pizza?" Mallory asked as they walked out of the hospital.

"There's a new place just a few blocks from here." Ashley pointed to the right. "With a view of the harbor."

"Perfect," Joy said. "And then, Eloise and Mallory, we'll need to walk to my place to get my car."

Ashley led the way to Concord Street and through the waterfront park. The girls ran ahead and then stopped at the Pineapple Fountain, their faces uplifted to the spray. Joy's heart swelled as Eloise reached for Mallory's hand.

"Aww," Ashley said. "I always wanted a sister. These two make me want one even more."

"Sabrina's an only child too."

"We've talked about that."

Joy didn't say anything more. The difference was Sabrina now had a family of her own, while Ashley had just lost her husband before ever having children.

When they reached the girls, Ashley said, "We'll turn left here."

A few minutes later they reached Amalfi's Pizza. After a short wait they were seated on the second floor next to an open window with a view of the harbor, including Fort Sumter.

Eloise pointed to the north. "The Cooper River flows into the bay that way." She pointed to the south. "And the Ashley River flows in from that way."

Mallory gave Ashley a questioning look. "Were you named after the river?"

Ashley grinned. "Yep. My mom named me after that muddy river that flows through swamps."

Mallory wrinkled her nose.

"I like swamps," Ashley said. "All sorts of amazing things live and grow in swamps."

"That's very true," Joy said.

"Like alligators?" Mallory asked.

"Sometimes," Ashley answered. "They aren't all over the place here like in Florida."

Joy shivered. Thankfully, that was true.

The waiter came and took their order. After he left, Mallory looked at Ashley and said, "Was your daddy okay with you being name after bad water?"

Joy bristled at Mallory's question but Ashley laughed.

"Muddy water," she said. "Not bad water."

Mallory giggled. "So was he?"

"Was who?"

"Was your daddy okay with your mom naming you after the river?"

"That's kind of a long story."

Mallory grinned at her. "Please tell us."

"Mallory." Joy realized Ashley was evading answering questions about her father. "Tell us about art camp. How did that go this week?"

Mallory didn't seem to notice that Joy had purposefully changed the subject. She happily told them all about art camp and what she'd made each day. A dream catcher on Monday, a woven pot holder on Tuesday, a mosaic on Wednesday, paper lanterns on Thursday. "And today we made a jar into a pencil holder."

"That sounds like fun," Joy said. "What are you doing with everything you made?"

"Keeping most of it—except I'll give the pot holder to Mommy and the pencil holder to Daddy, for Father's Day."

"Perfect," Joy responded.

Once the small pepperoni and margherita pizzas and Caesar salad arrived, the girls concentrated on eating while Ashley and Joy chatted.

"I really like your hair color," Ashley said. "A little lighter is great for summer."

Eloise nodded in agreement.

"Thank you," Joy said, and then changed the subject again. "I take it you and your mother are close to Hannah and Parker."

"That's right." Ashley speared a crouton in her salad. "They're like an aunt and uncle to me. I didn't have any family around except Mother and her grandfather, who died when I was ten. So Hannah and Parker, and then Lindsay, were always a big part of my life."

Joy thought about the Crane cousin that Evelyn had mentioned but didn't ask Ashley about him.

Eloise asked, "But what about your dad?" Obviously, Eloise hadn't noticed that Joy had purposefully changed the subject earlier either.

"We need to stop asking personal questions," Joy said.

"What does that mean?" Mallory shoved half a piece of pizza into her mouth.

"It means—"

Ashley interrupted Joy. "It's all right." She smiled at Mallory. "I never knew my dad."

Mallory's mouth fell open.

"Close your mouth, Sweetie," Joy said.

Ashley smiled again.

"Why didn't you know your dad?" Eloise asked.

Ashley shrugged. "I'm honestly not sure."

Eloise frowned. "I don't get it."

"Girls," Joy said, "Ashley's business is not our business. Don't ask any more personal questions."

Ashley smiled graciously as Eloise hung her head, while Mallory blurted out, "Oh, I also made a pencil today." Mallory seemed to have grown bored with the topic of Ashley's missing father. She grinned. "To go in the pencil jar."

"That's wonderful." Joy was pleased and relieved at the change of topic. "How in the world did you make a pencil?"

Mallory grinned. "We used twigs with a hole and glued lead in them."

Eloise didn't seem to hear Mallory and continued to stare at Ashley, but thankfully she didn't ask any more questions.

Twenty minutes later, as Joy signed the receipt, her phone jingled. *Sabrina.* "Excuse me," she said to Ashley and the girls. "I'm going to go ahead and answer this."

"Mom? Can you come back to the hospital?"

"Of course I can come. What's going on?"

"They're going to keep me overnight. Shirley won't say why. She said Dr. Barnhardt will talk to me in the next half hour or so. I'd feel better if you were here."

Ashley whispered loudly, "I can take the girls to my apartment. It's over the salon."

Joy wasn't sure the Crane Building was a safe place to be.

"Are you with Ashley?" Sabrina asked.

"Yes," Joy answered. "She came to dinner with us."

"I heard her offer. Take her up on it," Sabrina said. "Then you or Rob can take the girls home and put them to bed."

"All right." Joy tried to keep her voice even, to hide her worry. "I'll see you soon."

Chapter Four

Joy walked with Ashley and the girls to East Bay Street. Staring at the Crane Building, Joy spoke quietly to Ashley. "Do you think the building is safe after everything that happened today?"

"I understand your concern," Ashley answered. "But I'm positive my apartment is safe. I installed a security system before I moved in."

"Does your mother live above the salon too?"

Ashley shook her head. "She lives in her grandfather's old house."

Joy pursed her lips. Sabrina was all right with the girls going with Ashley. Surely they'd been to her friend's apartment before. "All right," Joy said.

When they reached the Crane Building, and after exchanging phone numbers, Ashley said, "Call me when you're ready to leave the hospital, and I'll walk the girls over."

"Thank you." Joy told her granddaughters goodbye and then stayed put as they went through the gate, which Ashley had just opened with a code. As the girls followed Ashley up the outside staircase, Joy sent a quick text to her sister, Hope. Sabrina was close to her aunt Hope and would want her to know what was going on. Don't freak

OUT, BUT SABRINA WAS HIT BY AN SUV. SHE'S DOING WELL, CONSIDERING. BUT SHE'S IN THE HOSPITAL. I'LL TEXT WHEN I KNOW MORE.

Hope texted right back. OH NO. I'M PRAYING. GIVE SABRINA A HUG. MAKE SURE AND LET ME KNOW AS SOON AS YOU KNOW SOMETHING.

Joy slipped her phone into her purse and hurried back to the hospital. When she reached Sabrina's room, Dr. Barnhardt had just entered. Sabrina appeared paler and more haggard than she had when Joy left. She pressed her left hand against the side of her face, and Joy wondered if the pain had spread.

"Hi, Mom," Sabrina said. "You haven't missed anything."

Rob sat in the chair, leaning forward. He appeared pale and haggard too.

Dr. Barnhardt waved at Joy. Then he turned to Sabrina. "How is your pain level?"

"My head is hurting more."

"No wonder," he said. "You have a subdural hematoma."

Rob sat up straight. "What is that, exactly?"

"The impact of Sabrina's head against the pavement, through the helmet, burst blood vessels. This caused blood to pool and push against the brain and caused it to swell. Hopefully the blood will be absorbed and the swelling will go down. We'll monitor it closely."

"What if the swelling doesn't go down?" Sabrina asked.

"Then we'll need to operate. For now, we'll move you up to the fourth floor, continue to observe you, and then do another CT scan in the morning." Dr. Barnhardt glanced from Sabrina to Rob to Joy and back to Sabrina. "Any other questions?"

"What would the surgery involve?" Sabrina asked.

"A neurosurgeon would do the surgery, of course. It would most likely be a craniotomy."

"Brain surgery?" Sabrina asked.

Dr. Barnhardt nodded.

Joy shivered.

"But," Dr. Barnhardt said, "we'll take this a step at a time. You'll be checked on throughout the night, and then the CT scan in the morning will give us a better idea. I've already contacted Dr. Reynolds, our best neurosurgeon. He'll stop by your room in the morning."

"All right," Sabrina said. "Is there any reason for my husband to stay with me tonight?"

"It's up to you," Dr. Barnhardt said, turning to Rob. "Sabrina won't get much rest no matter what. If you stay, you won't either. I know you have young children—you can't spread yourself too thin. It's better to pace yourself…"

Joy sat down in the open chair in the room.

"It's a good thing you didn't sit or stand up after you hit your head," Dr. Barnhardt said. "Whoever called 911 may have saved your life."

Sabrina sighed. "I thought I was okay, but Mom wouldn't let me get up. She insisted I get checked out."

Dr. Barnhardt glanced at Joy. "Good work." Then he said to Sabrina, "Transportation will be here in a few minutes to move you up to the fourth floor."

When the doctor left, Sabrina said to Rob, "I don't think you should stay. Go home with the girls and get them to bed. They'll be more settled if you do."

"I can stay with you," Joy said.

Sabrina shook her head. "I'll call you if I need you, but if they're going to check on me all night long you won't get any sleep either. I'd rather have you rested to watch the girls tomorrow."

"All right." Joy stood. "Do you want me to take the girls home now? And then you can come later, Rob?"

Sabrina reached for Rob's hand. "You should go soon."

"Okay," he said.

"I'll call Ashley to bring the girls over," Joy said, looking at Rob. "I'll sit with them in the waiting room until you're ready. And then I'll come to the house in the morning so you can come back up here."

Rob nodded but didn't say anything.

Joy stepped to the bed, leaned down, and kissed Sabrina on the forehead, saying another silent prayer as she did. "I love you, Sweetie."

"I love you too." Sabrina met Joy's eyes. "Would you ask Reverend Neal to put me on the prayer chain?"

"Of course," Joy answered. "I'll call while I'm waiting for the girls."

"I'll text you my room number," Sabrina said.

"Great." Joy patted Rob on the shoulder. "Take your time."

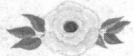

As Joy left a voice mail for the pastor of Sabrina's church, where Joy attended as well, the tremor in her voice gave away how worried she was. She said she'd call with an update in the morning and then said goodbye.

Then she texted Hope with the latest news.

PRAYING! Hope texted back.

Joy exhaled just as Shirley appeared and sat down beside her.

Shirley put her arm around Joy. "How are you holding up?"

"I'm all right. Trying not to worry. Do you think she'll need surgery?"

Shirley squeezed Joy's shoulder. "There's no way to know at this point, but I'd say the majority of people with hematomas do."

"That's helpful," Joy said.

"And by far, the majority who have surgery recover. It's the ones who never come to the hospital that we truly worry about. She's exactly where she needs to be."

Joy leaned against Shirley's shoulder. "That's reassuring."

"Can I pray for Sabrina and you?" Shirley asked.

"Please." Joy bowed her head.

Shirley prayed for healing for Sabrina, strength for Joy, and comfort for all of them. As she said, "Amen" Joy raised her head. Dr. Barnhardt stood by the desk. He smiled at her.

Shirley let go of Joy and stood. "Text me anytime if you have a question or need someone to talk to. I don't want you to worry too much."

Just then Rebekah Osborne, a detective with the Charleston Police Department, stepped through the sliding doors into the waiting room. Joy stood, sure she'd come with information about the hit-and-run.

But when Parker Hollingsworth blurted out, "What took you so long?" it was obvious which case Rebekah was investigating.

"I got here as soon as I could, Parker. I have several cases I'm working on today." Rebekah appeared tired and a little stressed. "How is Hannah?"

"Miserable. It's not every day your best friend tries to poison you with her signature hair dye."

Rebekah didn't respond to that. "I meant, how is her health?"

He shrugged. "They're still running tests to see what damage has been done—and what exactly Sassie used to poison her."

"I need to speak with Hannah," Rebekah said.

Parker stepped in front of Joy and Shirley as he continued to speak to Rebekah. "Come on back to her room." He motioned to the hallway and boomed, "Come on back."

"You need to tone it down, Parker," Rebekah said. "And not make accusations."

"Not speak the truth?" he bellowed. "Says who?"

Joy stayed quiet, but once Rebekah and Parker were down the hall, Shirley rolled her eyes and said, "I'm not sure if that man can stop talking. Listening to him go on and on for the last couple of hours is about more than I can take, and that's saying a lot."

"Bless you," Joy said. "I don't know how you do it."

"Believe me, the patients usually aren't the problems. Family—and sometimes friends—are the big challenge." She stood and winked. "But this too shall pass."

Joy nodded. That was good advice for anyone in the emergency room, patient or visitor.

Shirley returned to work, and a few minutes later Ashley came through the door with Eloise and Mallory. Both girls looked worried.

"Is Mommy okay?" Eloise asked.

"Yes," Joy answered, "but she needs to spend the night so the doctors and nurses can observe her."

Mallory slipped her hand into Joy's. "What about Daddy?"

"He's going to go home with you. Then, in the morning, I'll come over so he can come back up to the hospital."

"Can we see Mommy?" Eloise asked.

"Not tonight," Joy said.

Tears filled Eloise's eyes. "Will Mommy come home tomorrow?"

"Hopefully," Joy said. "If not, we'll ask if you can see her then."

Mallory squeezed Joy's hand. Joy squeezed it back and then wrapped her free arm around Eloise. Ashley took a step away from the girls. "Thank you so much," Joy said to her.

"Of course," Ashley said. "Let me know if there's anything I can do tomorrow."

Before Joy could respond, Rob came toward them. Both girls let go of Joy and ran to their father.

After he hugged them, he said, "Say good night to Mimi."

Joy hugged the girls. "I'll see you soon."

"Bye, Mimi," Eloise whispered.

Mallory squeezed her extra hard and then the two left with Rob.

Once they'd gone through the sliding doors, Ashley asked, "How is Sabrina doing?"

Tears welled in Joy's eyes. "She has a subdural hematoma from hitting her head on the asphalt. They don't know if she'll need surgery yet or not."

"That makes sense that they're keeping her overnight."

Joy agreed. "They're moving her up to the fourth floor. They'll monitor her closely, waking her up every half hour. Then they'll do another CT scan in the morning."

"Ashley!" Parker came toward them, followed by Rebekah, who was walking quickly to keep up with him. "Rebekah needs to search the salon."

"Parker." Rebekah's voice was low and firm. "You need to stop. This is not your investigation."

Parker kept talking to Ashley. "If your mother had nothing to do with Hannah's poisoning, then you'll let Rebekah search the shop, right?"

"Parker." Rebekah's voice grew louder. "Knock it off."

Parker crossed his arms after shoving his rolled sleeves up to his biceps.

Ashley stared at him. "If anyone wants to search the salon, they'll need to get a warrant."

Parker shook his head and then with disgust in his voice said, "Is this what it's come to?"

Ashley squared her shoulders. "What are you talking about?"

"Our families. What your mother has done is going to tear us apart."

After Parker retreated to Hannah's room, Rebekah sat down next to Ashley. "May I ask you a few questions?"

"As long as you're not asking to search Mother's business without a warrant."

"I'm not," Rebekah answered.

"All right then."

Joy stood. "I'll get going."

"I'd rather that you stayed," Ashley said. "You were in the salon when Hannah lost consciousness. You can back me up on what happened."

Joy glanced at Rebekah.

"That's fine."

Joy sat back down.

"Parker's accusation is serious."

"What does the toxicology report show?" Ashley asked. "Was Hannah even poisoned?"

"The report isn't back yet, but her kidneys are damaged, which is a sign of poisoning."

"Then what's the point of suspecting that Mother poisoned Hannah if there's no actual evidence that she was poisoned?"

Rebekah laced her fingers together. "Parker seems to think your mother had a motive."

"Parker thinks a lot of things." Ashley squared her shoulders. "Have you done any research into hair dye? I don't see how something that's applied to hair could be absorbed into the body fast enough to knock someone out like that."

"There have been cases of that type of poisoning over a long period of time," Rebekah said.

"Then it would have been coincidental that Hannah collapsed this afternoon, in the shop?"

Rebekah nodded. "Most likely. Or there's the possibility of mixing something toxic into the dye that would cause a reaction or a gas that the victim breathes in."

"If there was a gas, wouldn't it have impacted Mother?" Ashley asked. "And Joy too?"

Rebekah had a questioning look on her face.

Joy explained. "Not only was I in the salon, but I was in the chair next to Hannah."

"Oh."

Ashley asked, her voice a little snarky, "Hannah didn't tell you that?"

Rebekah shook her head. "But Parker did the talking." She sighed. "Do you think there's a possibility that your mother might have done anything to harm Hannah?"

"Her best friend since high school? Never. Mother might be driven and ruthless in business, but she'd never harm anyone. Especially not Hannah Hollingsworth."

"Parker says their relationship isn't as straightforward as it seems. He says they had problems back in their early twenties that have recently put a strain on their relationship."

Ashley laughed, wryly. "Sorry, I don't have any memory of them having problems. I was a baby when they were in their early twenties."

"Have you made any progress on the safe that was stolen from Sassie?" Joy asked. "And who hit Sabrina?"

"I'm not working on those cases."

"Has anyone looked into a connection between the three incidents?" Joy couldn't hide the concern in her voice. "All happened within an hour in or near the Crane Building."

"I'll look at the other two cases and consider that." Rebekah stood. "And I'll get a warrant to search the shop. Plus, Ashley, I need to question your mother. I'll stop by the shop and do that in the morning."

Ashley didn't respond.

"I'll be in touch soon," Rebekah said and then headed for the exit.

Ashley remained silent.

Finally, Joy asked, "Are you okay?"

"Yes." Ashley stood. "Did you know Mother cuts Rebekah's hair too? She also cuts Parker's hair."

Joy stood also. "I'll walk you back to your place."

Ashley shook her head. "No. I'm going to walk you home. I insist."

"It's only two blocks," Joy said.

"Well, I'm only across the street." Ashley tilted her head. "I win."

As they stepped out the door of the hospital and then headed east, Joy turned and caught sight of the evening sun through the buildings. Pink and orange streaked across the sky. Ahead of them was a group of young women, all dressed up.

Ashley sighed. "I remember Friday nights when I was in my early twenties."

Joy smiled. "Charleston had to have been a fun town to grow up in. Did you know Barry then?"

"We knew each other from college, but we didn't start dating until we were twenty-seven. He moved to town from Atlanta to work for a tech firm. We got together for dinner and then married a year later."

"Aww," Joy said. "That's so sweet. I really am sorry, Ashley. Losing a husband is hard no matter what, but it's a horrible sadness to go through in your early thirties."

"Thank you," Ashley said. "You and Sabrina have both been so understanding."

The young women ahead of them turned right, into Bedons Alley, which led to Elliot Street. Their laughter rang out into the warm night.

Ashley smiled. "It's good to hear people happy."

"Yes," Joy said. "It really is."

"I'm worried about Mother," Ashley said. "She doesn't have a lot of support, and Parker speaking out against her is upsetting. His opinion has power in this town."

"How so?" Joy asked.

"He's a developer. He's wealthy. He's respected."

"Your mom is respected."

"Not in the same way," Ashley said. "It's hard to explain. But Parker is part of the establishment here. People listen to him. To have him accusing Mother in public like that is unsettling, especially when she's been close to both Hannah and Parker for decades."

"Why would Parker accuse her of trying to hurt Hannah?"

"Oh, I'm sure he believes his accusations. I'm sure he believes he's absolutely right. This is minor compared to Sabrina being hit, but Parker's reaction could be bad for our business, especially when we're expanding the spa and planning the reopening in two weeks." Ashley paused a moment. "They've all been friends for so long—they used to call themselves the Dream Team."

"Your mom and Hannah were talking about that this afternoon."

"Really?"

"Yes," Joy answered. "In middle school, they called themselves the Dare to Dream Team."

"I hadn't heard that before," Ashley said. "It all sounds so dorky, but it makes more sense that they started it in middle school."

Joy slowed her pace. "They said they had big aspirations."

"I bet they did." Ashley shook her head. "It's really hard to see Parker so upset with Mother."

"Ashley!"

A girl with long hair, wearing a sundress and sandals, crossed Church Street and was coming toward them. "Ashley!" she yelled again.

"Lindsay?"

The girl started running, and then Ashley began jogging. "What's going on?" the girl asked as she fell into Ashley's arms.

"I'm not sure. Where have you been?"

"Jenna's house. Dad texted me and told me to stay with her—that Mom was in the hospital and he'd come get me. But he hasn't answered a text in the last hour. Is Mom okay?"

"I think so," Ashley said. "We just came from the hospital. We saw your dad a few minutes ago. He didn't say that she wasn't okay."

Lindsay let go of Ashley. "Why is Daddy accusing Auntie Sassie of trying to poison Mom?"

Ashley shook her head. "He's upset. Your mom has been through quite an ordeal."

Lindsay pointed to the hospital. "I'm going to go talk to Daddy right now. We need to work this out—we all need to get together and talk."

Ashley smiled at the girl. "Go see your mom and talk with your dad," she said. "And then text me and let me know if they want to talk. I'll do my best to get Mother to do the same." Ashley glanced at

Joy. "I'd like you to meet Joy Atkins. Her daughter, Sabrina, is a good friend of mine."

"Pleased to meet you," Lindsay said. "I'm Parker and Hannah Hollingsworth's daughter."

"I'm pleased to meet you too." Joy turned to Ashley. "Walk back to the hospital with Lindsay. My house is right here." She pointed to the right.

"Okay," Ashley said. "Let me know how Sabrina is doing in the morning."

"I will," Joy said. "Good night."

"Good night," Ashley and Lindsay said in unison.

Joy walked up her brick-lined pathway, past the flower beds she'd put in and planted with Carolina jessamine and rain lilies. She unlocked the front door and went into the house. The scent of the lavender on the dining room table greeted her, and she inhaled and then exhaled slowly. There truly was no place like home.

Her urban two-story house in Charleston was so different from her rambling three-story, suburban home back in Houston. But it was perfect for her now. She put her purse on the table and locked the door behind her. Then she headed straight out the back door and to the bench Wilson had made that she had moved from Houston and given an honorary spot in her Charleston backyard. Joy had placed it under the magnolia tree, whose green leaves continued to shine even in the waning light.

Her heart began to race. They'd come close to another horrible tragedy.

She'd gotten through the worst of her grief over losing Wilson. Usually what she felt now was a deep appreciation for his life and the years they'd had together, but having Sabrina be the victim of a hit-and-run brought back her grief for Wilson. One of her worst fears was losing Sabrina too.

Her phone rang. Joy expected it to be Sabrina or Rob. But it was Evelyn. Joy answered with a quick, "Hello, Ev."

"I heard about Sabrina," Evelyn said. "Is she all right?"

"I think so." Joy explained the diagnosis and that surgery might be necessary.

"I also heard about Hannah Hollingsworth. There's a rumor going around that Sassie Crane poisoned her and you were there when it happened. Is that true?"

Joy sputtered. "Yes, I was there, but no, I don't think that's true at all." But she wasn't sure she sounded very convincing.

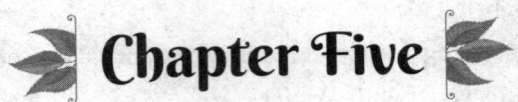

Chapter Five

Joy slept fitfully, waking up to the image of Sabrina flying over the hood of the SUV and onto the pavement over and over. She felt immense relief that Sabrina was alive, mixed with fear of what the morning might bring and anger at whoever had hit her—and then fled the scene.

Finally at five, she crawled out of bed and shuffled down the stairs. Her coffeepot wasn't set to start until six—it was Saturday after all—so she hit the on button and stared at it as the coffee began to brew.

She was tempted to text Sabrina to see how she was but stopped herself. If Sabrina was asleep, the last thing she wanted to do was wake her up.

Still in her nightgown and robe, Joy took her coffee up to the piazza on the second floor, where she'd have a glimpse of the sunrise over the bay. She sat on the bistro-style chair and put her mug on the round table, staring to the east over the top of the house across the street. Below, by the light of the streetlamp, she could see a seagull hop along the sidewalk. The sky was still dark.

Even with her eyes open, the image of Sabrina flying over the hood of the vehicle popped into Joy's head again. She said another prayer, asking God to heal Sabrina without her having to have surgery. Joy's entire world had turned upside down when Wilson died. The thought of losing her only child—her daughter—was more than she could bear. She couldn't go there. She had to stay in the moment and as far away from the past and future as possible.

The first light of morning began to filter through the darkness. The streetlights blinked off just as a streak of lavender rose above the house across the street. Then the darkness became a pale blue and the light began to spread, lifting Joy's spirits. The gull flew up and called out as it moved east.

Her phone dinged in her robe pocket. Joy pulled it out, again expecting Sabrina or Rob. It was Hope. HAVE YOU HEARD ANYTHING?

NO. BUT THANKS FOR CHECKING.

ARE YOU UP FOR A PHONE CALL?

SURE.

As soon as her phone rang, Joy answered it.

"How are you doing?" Hope asked.

Tears welled in Joy's eyes and filled her voice. "Worried about Sabrina."

"Of course you are."

Hope listened as Joy gave her the details of the accident and what the doctor said. When she finished, Hope said, "I'm so sorry that Sabrina is going through this and you are too. You must be beside yourself."

Joy swallowed hard. It meant a lot that her sister acknowledged her worry. "I'll admit, I am worried."

"I'm praying for both Sabrina and you. Make sure and let me know when you find out anything."

"I will." Joy hesitated a moment and then said, "Do you have time for me to tell you about another case that may or may not be related to Sabrina's hit-and-run?"

"Of course I do."

"It's all confidential."

Hope laughed. "I can keep a secret. I'm not five anymore."

Joy told her about Hannah collapsing in the salon and then Sassie claiming the safe had been stolen from the warehouse section of the Crane Building that was being remodeled into spa space. "Sassie thinks whoever stole the safe hit Sabrina."

"Wow, what a crazy chain of events," Hope said.

"I know."

"Is Hannah ill?"

"She's in the hospital." Joy hesitated. "Her husband thinks Sassie poisoned her."

"*Parker* thinks that?"

"You know Parker?"

"Yes. I worked with him when the college expanded the student center. He was the developer—they wanted my ideas as far as the landscaping."

"That sounds like a small project for him, from what I've heard," Joy said.

"I think he got a tax write-off."

Joy smiled. "What did you think of him?"

"Nice guy, overall. Pretty talkative. Seems to know the business and wants everyone to know he does." Hope paused just a moment and then said, "He seems to be used to getting his way. He went toe to toe with the president—and won."

"Interesting," Joy said. No doubt Parker Hollingsworth was used to controlling situations.

"Let me know how I can help," Hope said. "I can stay with the girls. Do laundry. Help with the yard. Help you. Whatever you and Sabrina need."

"Thank you," Joy said, sincerely meaning it.

As she ended the call, Joy felt better. She and her sister, who was four years younger than Joy, had had their conflicts in the past. But since Hope moved to Charleston their relationship had improved. Hope was a big fan of Sabrina's. It was nice to have her on Joy's team now too.

Joy sipped her coffee as the warmth of the sun reached the piazza. It was supposed to be a hot and sticky day—eighty-seven degrees with high humidity.

She drank the last of the coffee and then headed inside for her shower.

A half hour later she sat at her kitchen table with her phone in her hand, anxious to hear from Sabrina. Finally, she texted Rob. I'M ON MY WAY OVER TO FIX THE GIRLS BREAKFAST.

Rob texted back immediately. THANK YOU. I'LL LEAVE FOR THE HOSPITAL AS SOON AS YOU ARRIVE.

Joy replied with, HAVE YOU HEARD ANYTHING FROM SABRINA?

JUST THAT HER HEADACHE IS WORSE. SHE HASN'T SEEN THE DOCTOR YET THIS MORNING.

Joy gripped her phone as she inhaled deeply. Then she sent Sabrina a text. GOOD MORNING. I'M ON MY WAY TO YOUR HOUSE. ARE YOU FEELING BETTER?

Sabrina replied, I'M DOING ALL RIGHT. GIVE THE GIRLS LOTS OF LOVE AND HUGS.

Joy replied with a smiley face. It wouldn't do any good to let Sabrina know how worried she was. She'd focus on what she needed to do. Go take care of the girls so Rob could get to the hospital.

Eloise was getting too old for animal hotcakes, but Mallory still loved them. "Here comes a camel," Joy announced as she slid it off the griddle.

Mallory, who wore a Wonder Woman cape over her pajamas, called out, "I'll take it!" She held up her plate.

After Joy delivered it, she asked Eloise what she would like.

"Just a round one, please."

"You betcha," Joy said. "Give me a minute."

Mallory touched the camel and then licked syrup off her finger. "I can't wait to cut into it." She grinned.

Eloise took a sip of her orange juice. "Mimi, you should take a picture first."

"Of course." Joy pulled her phone from her pocket. Mallory positioned her dish and grinned again.

After Joy took the photo, Mallory said, "Would you please send it to Mommy?"

"I sure will." Joy sent the text and then spoke to Eloise. "I'll take a photo of you to send to your mom too."

"I don't want to," Eloise said.

"All right." Joy slipped her phone back into her pocket and returned to the griddle. The girls, four years apart, were at very different stages in life.

Later, as she finished the dishes and the girls tidied up their rooms, her phone dinged. It was Rob. SABRINA REMINDED ME THAT THE GIRLS HAVE A BIRTHDAY PARTY TO GO TO AT 11.

I CAN TAKE THEM, Joy texted back.

IT'S A COWORKER'S DAUGHTER. I'LL TAKE THEM. BUT CAN YOU COME SIT WITH SABRINA?

OF COURSE. DO THE GIRLS HAVE A GIFT TO TAKE?

NO. WE WERE GOING TO GET IT THIS MORNING.

I'LL TAKE THE GIRLS SHOPPING, Joy texted. ANY IDEAS? GUIDELINES?

EIGHT-YEAR-OLD GIRL WHO LOVES ARTS AND CRAFTS. ELOISE WILL HAVE SOME GOOD IDEAS.

Once the girls finished tidying their rooms, Joy took them to the craft store in downtown Charleston, where the girls chose a bracelet spinning loom. Next, they stopped by the stationery store for a card and gift bag. By the time they returned home, Rob's car was in the driveway.

As the girls ran to the house, Rob came out the front door to meet them. Joy quickly searched his face, looking for any sign of how Sabrina might be doing. He swept Mallory up into his arms.

"How is Mommy?" Eloise asked.

"The same." Rob shifted Mallory to one arm and pulled Eloise close. "Which is good news."

Eloise leaned against him.

"We'll be back here by one," Rob said to Joy.

"All right," she answered. "I'll meet you here then."

Fifteen minutes later she was at the hospital. When she approached Sabrina's door, she heard voices. Expecting a nurse or doctor, Joy pushed open the door to find Rebekah at the foot of Sabrina's bed.

"You didn't see the driver?" The detective held a small notebook in her hand.

Sabrina answered, "No. It happened so fast—all I saw was a black vehicle."

"Did anyone get a license plate number?"

"Hello," Joy said.

Sabrina smiled when she saw her. "Hi."

"Hello, Joy," Rebekah said. "I was just asking Sabrina about the accident."

"Mom, do you know if anyone got a license plate number?"

Joy shook her head. "One of the witnesses said there wasn't a plate on the front. There was one on the back, but no one got it as the SUV sped around the corner." She turned to Rebekah. "Have you been able to get any security footage from nearby businesses?"

"We're working on that." Rebekah made a note in her notebook. "As of now, we have no leads. I'll check the police report, but did you happen to get any of the witnesses' names?"

"Yes," Joy answered. "One was a young man who works in transportation here. His name is Lance."

"Great." Rebekah closed her notebook. "I'll go see if he's working."

After Rebekah left the room, Joy sat down in the chair next to Sabrina's bed. "Any better?"

Sabrina shrugged. "The same."

"What did the doctor say?"

"He ordered another CT scan. I should have it soon." Sabrina closed her eyes. "I think it's just a precaution. Hopefully, I'll be able to go home by this afternoon."

Joy wasn't sure if she hoped for that. She wanted the doctor to be as cautious as needed. She didn't say that though. Instead, she said, "Anne mentioned that Addie is doing the same sports camp as the girls."

Sabrina nodded.

"She said she'll pick them up on Monday, and they can play with Addie."

"Oh, I'll be home by then."

"Even if you are, you still might want her to pick them up."

"That's true," Sabrina said, her eyes still closed. "Thanks. I'll send her a text."

"Auntie Hope sends her love and prayers."

Sabrina smiled. "That's nice."

"Knock, knock."

Joy turned toward the door, where Anne stood, a concerned expression on her face.

"Come on in," Sabrina called out.

Anne stepped into the room. "What's the latest?" she asked Sabrina.

After Sabrina gave her an update, Anne looked closely at Joy. "How are you holding up?"

"I'm okay," Joy said. "Relieved that Sabrina is getting such good care."

"Want to grab coffee this afternoon with Evelyn and me?" Anne asked. "Lili took Addie to her riding lesson. I have some errands to run but will be back around two."

Joy lowered her voice, "Thanks, but I'm going to pass."

"Let me know if you change your mind," Anne said.

After Anne left, Sabrina said, "Mom, you should have coffee with them. I'll be fine."

"I can have coffee with them anytime," Joy said. "I'd rather be available to you."

Sabrina frowned at her. "You need to get your own stuff done." Then she closed her eyes, and Joy sat quietly, allowing Sabrina to rest, until another knock fell on the door.

Sabrina opened her eyes. "Come in."

Ashley stepped into the room. "Hey, you two. How's it going?"

"No change." Sabrina sat up straighter and smiled. "How are you?"

"Good," Ashley answered. "I'm on my lunch break and thought I'd check in. Any word on who hit you?"

Sabrina shook her head.

"How about on who stole the safe?" Joy asked.

"No," Ashley said.

"What about Hannah? How is she?"

Ashley gestured to the door. "She's on this floor too. Just down the hall. They're keeping her for observation."

"Sounds familiar." Sabrina seemed frustrated.

"How is Lindsay?" Joy asked.

"Okay." Ashley shrugged. "At least she was last night. I haven't heard from her yet this morning, but she's probably still sleeping."

Joy smiled at Ashley. "And your mother?"

"Quiet," Ashley answered. "She canceled all of her appointments for today and hasn't responded to any of my texts. I'm going to go check on her before I go back to the shop."

"Mom, you should go with Ashley."

Joy thought she should stay with Sabrina and started to say so as someone else knocked on the door. "Transportation."

"Come in," Joy called out.

Lance stepped into the room. He grinned.

"Hello," Joy said. "Did Detective Osborne find you?"

"Yes, ma'am," he said. "I answered all of her questions." He turned to Sabrina. "You ready for your scan?"

"As ready as I'll ever be."

Ashley said to Sabrina, "I'm going to head over to Mother's house. I'll text you later this afternoon."

"Sounds good." Sabrina looked at Joy. "Mom, go with Ashley. Sassie might remember something about the SUV that hit me. Or have an idea of who might have taken her safe."

"I should stay here."

"But I'm going to get my CT scan. You'll be back before I am."

"The scan will take a while," Lance said.

Joy hesitated. No doubt Sabrina wouldn't be back in the room for a while. And Joy did hope Sassie might have an idea of who took her safe—and hit Sabrina.

"Do you want me to go with you?" Joy asked Ashley.

"Sure," she answered.

"The walk will do you good," Sabrina said. "Please go."

"All right." Joy stood. "Sabrina, text me if you need me sooner. I'll be back before you know it."

Sassie's house was four blocks away, on a corner lot. Joy guessed the Crane House was built in the late eighteenth century. It was a gray adobe with a white wooden piazza on both the ground and second floor in the back of the house.

Ashley led the way to the alley and opened the back wrought iron gate, which led to a brick courtyard lined with palmetto trees. Joy followed her to a side door. They stepped into a mudroom and then a modern kitchen with a tile floor, granite countertops, and an island in the middle.

"Mother!" Ashley called.

When no one answered, she called out, "Where are you?"

Joy heard a faint voice answer, "In the sunroom."

Ashley led the way into a hallway and then around an open staircase and into a living room with plush velvet furniture.

"Back here." Sassie sat in the sunroom off the living room on a wicker settee with one leg tucked underneath her, staring at the coffee cup on the table in front of her.

"What are you doing?" Ashley asked.

Sassie kept her eyes on the mug. "Nothing."

Ashley stood in the doorway, with Joy right behind her. "Why didn't you answer my calls?"

Sassie patted the cushion next to her and then her pants pockets. "I'm not sure where my phone is."

"You canceled your appointments," Ashley said. "Didn't answer your phone. Didn't reply to any of my texts. I've been worried. What's going on?"

Sassie raised her head. "I'm taking the day off, is all."

"You never take a day off."

"Then it's about time, right?"

"No. Not when I had to reschedule all of your appointments for you, which is no easy feat considering how tight you pack your schedule. And not when Hannah is still in the hospital and Lindsay doesn't understand what's going on. Not when Parker is on a rampage." Ashley crossed her arms. "I need your help."

Sassie picked up the mug, which had a sailboat on it and the words GREETINGS FROM CHARLESTON. "I don't think there's much I can do about any of that." She looked past Ashley at Joy. "How is Sabrina doing?"

"Hanging in there," Joy said.

"How about Hannah?" Ashley asked her mother. "Have you heard from her? Or Parker?"

"No," Sassie said.

"Because you haven't checked your phone."

Sassie shrugged.

"So much for the Dream Team," Ashley muttered as she marched past Joy and through the living room.

Sassie stood and said to Joy, "I'm sorry Ashley pulled you into this."

Joy concentrated on why she'd accompanied Ashley. "I was hoping to find out more about who might have stolen your safe and hit Sabrina. Have you thought of anything that could help the investigation?"

Sassie shook her head and answered vaguely, "I've put a lot of thought into it...."

"And?" Joy asked.

Sassie took a sip of her coffee.

Joy was beginning to feel as frustrated as Ashley.

Sassie smiled. "Would you like me to cut your hair now? I can do it here."

Joy shook her head. "Monday will be fine. I need to get back to the hospital soon."

Ashley returned to the sunroom, holding up Sassie's phone. "You've missed a text from Hannah, two calls from Parker, and a text from Lindsay. Mother, you need to think of our business. I can't afford another financial hit."

Sassie reached for her phone. "I'll take that."

Ashley handed the phone over, although she seemed reluctant to do so. "We have the grand opening to think of. Remember? If we don't watch out, Parker could ruin everything."

"Don't worry about it." Sassie clutched the phone.

Ashley seemed to be searching her mother's eyes. "What is going on with you?"

"Nothing," Sassie said. "I just need some space. Some time to myself."

"Well, you need to call Hannah and Parker back."

"Parker isn't being very nice," Sassie answered. "He's threatening to sue me."

Ashley stepped forward and put her hand on her mother's shoulder. "Try to work with him. We don't want the salon and spa to go bankrupt. The last thing we need is for Parker to get even more upset."

"There's nothing I can do to make him less upset," Sassie said.

"Hannah mentioned that Parker is on new medication," Joy said. "Could that be contributing to his actions?"

"I have no idea," Sassie answered.

Ashley crossed her arms. "How about answering Parker's calls? You could ask him about his new medication."

Sassie rolled her eyes. "How about glasses of tea for the two of you? Would you do that for me, darlin'?"

It was Ashley's turn to roll her eyes. "We only have a few minutes, but I suppose we could take time for some tea. You don't want any?"

"I'll stick with my coffee."

Ashley stepped back from her mother and motioned to Joy. "You two sit. I'll just be a minute."

After Ashley left, Sassie returned to her seat and patted the arm of the chair next to the settee. "Please sit down," she said.

Joy obliged.

They sat in silence for a few minutes until Sassie finally said, "I really am sorry that Sabrina was hit and that somehow that old safe is involved."

"Tell me about the safe," Joy said.

"It belonged to my grandfather and at least his father before him. Perhaps even his grandfather."

"Was it still usable?"

Sassie nodded. "Granddaddy had a key to it, but he said it was empty."

Sassie gazed past Joy, into the living room. Then she stood again. Ashley approached with two glasses of sweet tea on a tray. "Thank you, darlin'," Sassie said. She put her mug down, took the tray, and placed it on the coffee table. Then she handed one glass to Joy and the other to Ashley.

Joy took a drink of tea and then said to Ashley, "We were just talking about the safe that was stolen."

"Really?" Ashley stared at her mother, but Sassie stayed silent. Finally, Ashley said, "Mother?"

"I found it in the warehouse a few days ago when one of the workers pulled down a false wall. I hadn't seen it in thirty-five years."

"Do you know the story of the safe?" Joy asked. "Did your grandfather keep anything particular in it?"

Sassie shook her head. "He said it was empty and gave it to me when I opened my shop. I kept it around for my customers for something to put their coffee cups on. But then one day it just disappeared. I heard my cousin took it. It seems he had a key to both my shop and the safe, but I never got the chance to ask back then, and later I didn't care to check. It no longer mattered."

"Can you elaborate?" Joy asked.

Sassie stared straight ahead. "No. I can't."

 Chapter Six

As she closed the wrought iron gate behind them, Ashley said, "I hate to say this, but I'm pretty sure Mother is hiding something."

Joy felt the same way, but she didn't know Sassie well enough to be sure about it. Perhaps she was simply distraught over the conflict with Parker and the missing safe. Joy said, "I know this sort of thing takes a while. And Detective Osborne seemed tired last night by the time she came to the hospital. It sounds as if she's working on multiple cases."

"You're right." Ashley sighed. "Do you think Hannah's poisoning, the stolen safe, and the hit-and-run are all connected?"

"Well, we know the stolen safe and the hit-and-run may have been. I don't know about a connection with Hannah's poisoning. That could be coincidental."

Ashley sighed. "But maybe not."

Joy agreed. "If your mother is being secretive, we need to determine what about, what her motivation is, and if it's connected to one or all three of the incidents that happened yesterday."

"What can we do?"

"Talk to your mother again. See if she is hiding something. Try to find out what's going on with her."

"She's always been evasive," Ashley said. "I doubt she'll give me a straight answer."

"Not even if we confront her?"

"Want to go back and ask her even more pointed questions?" Ashley suggested.

"I should get back to Sabrina."

"I'll go see if I can pry anything out of Mother."

"Good," Joy said. "And I'll talk to Lance again. I'll also stop in and say hello to Hannah, see how she's doing. As far as the safe, who else besides your mother knew it had been found?"

Ashley shrugged. "I have no idea. Maybe the contractor."

"Would she have told any of her relatives?"

Ashley shook her head. "There aren't any relatives around for her to tell."

"Do you know Evelyn Perry?"

"Of course," Ashley said.

"She thought she saw your mother's cousin in the lobby of the hospital yesterday about the same time your mom rushed into the gift shop like she was trying to hide from someone. The man had gray hair and a goatee."

Ashley frowned. "I don't know of any cousins."

"Evelyn said his name is Ernest Crane and that she hasn't seen him in over thirty years."

"Interesting." Ashley's eyes grew large. "That could have something to do with Mother being secretive."

Joy nodded. "I'll do some research on Ernest Crane and see if Evelyn has any more information."

"The Hollingsworths are wealthy and prominent members of the community," Ashley said. "Parker has a big mouth, which seems to be getting louder as he gets older. I'm afraid he'll turn people against Mother."

"Your mom is held in high esteem too," Joy said.

"But she doesn't hold the power the Hollingsworths do," Ashley said. "I don't think she realizes that. She's usually so good with interpersonal relationships, but she's off her game. She's making things worse by not seeing Hannah or answering Parker's calls or going to work. She looks suspicious."

"People aren't guilty because they act strangely."

"That's true," Ashley said. "It's not that I don't think Detective Osborne isn't working on this, but she has other cases. Like you said, she's busy. I'm hoping we can speed things up."

"Me too." Joy desperately wanted to know who hit Sabrina. She hoped looking into Hannah's supposed poisoning and the theft of the safe would help her find the hit-and-run driver.

Ashley turned back to her mother's house. "Text me if you find anything. If I haven't heard from you by the time I close the shop, I'll text you. And let me know right away if anything with Sabrina changes."

"Will do," Joy said and then hurried back to the hospital.

On her way through the lobby she googled *Ernest Crane, Charleston, South Carolina.*

Samuel Ernest Dixon popped up. Then Ernest Cook. Joy scrolled through similar listings. Finally, on the third page, "Charles Ernest Crane" was listed. She clicked on the link. There seemed to be something in the archives for the *Charleston Gazette* from 1988, but Joy couldn't access the link.

She reached the elevator and tucked her phone back into her purse. When she arrived on the fourth floor, she headed straight to Sabrina's room, but Sabrina wasn't back yet. She kept going, down to Hannah's room. She listened for a moment, didn't hear anything, and then knocked.

"Come in."

Joy stepped in and said, "I'm Joy Atkins. I met you yesterday at Sassie's."

Hannah smiled. "I remember you." Her auburn hair was piled high on her head, and her face appeared gaunt. "Your hair color turned out really well. Sassie always does such a good job."

Joy smiled. "How are you feeling?"

"All right. They ran more tests this morning. My kidney function isn't great—that's why they think it's a possibility I was poisoned." Hannah motioned to the chair beside the bed.

Joy sat down. "I heard your husband in the lobby last night saying that you'd been poisoned."

Hannah blushed. "I wish he wouldn't do that and especially not accuse Sassie. She didn't do anything to hurt me."

"Is there anyone you think might poison you?"

Hannah shook her head.

"A motive?"

She frowned. "To get back at Parker for running his big mouth around town?" Hannah hesitated for a moment and then said, "I appreciate you stopping by, but I'm a little tired."

"Oh, I'm sorry." Joy stood. "I just wanted to check on you."

"It's okay. And thank you," Hannah said. "I appreciate it."

"Take care." Joy started for the door.

"Wait," Hannah said.

Joy turned.

"Is it your daughter who was hit yesterday afternoon? Who kept Sassie from getting to the hospital?"

"Yes," Joy said.

"I'm sorry that happened."

"Thank you."

"How is she?" Hannah asked.

"All right. She's getting another CT scan right now."

Hannah smiled. "I hope everything works out okay."

"Thank you." Joy smiled back. "I was with Ashley last night and met your daughter, Lindsay. She seems like a wonderful young woman."

Hannah smiled more broadly. "She is. She should be here soon."

"Oh, good," Joy said. "I'll let you rest."

"Come back later if you like," Hannah said. "Although hopefully I'll be going home soon."

As Joy slipped out the door, she wondered if Rebekah had looked into other possibilities as far as Hannah being poisoned. What did she have for lunch yesterday? What did she drink? What was in the bottle she had with her? Joy wondered where the bottle ended up. The last she remembered, it had fallen to the floor. She didn't remember anyone picking it up.

Maybe Ashley knew what had happened to it.

When Joy returned to Sabrina's room, Lance was repositioning her bed. "Hello," Joy said to both of them.

"Perfect timing," Sabrina said.

"How did it go?" Joy asked.

"Better. I wasn't as nervous this time," Sabrina said.

Joy glanced at Sabrina and then back at Lance. "I know Detective Osborne already questioned you—but do you mind me asking you a couple of questions too?"

He shook his head. "Not at all."

"Do you remember anything more from yesterday? Any more details about the SUV that hit Sabrina?"

He shook his head. "The windows were tinted except for the windshield. I don't remember any bumper stickers on the front or back—but I might not have noticed. It looked like a security vehicle or something like that. Like I said, it didn't have a front license plate, and I didn't notice a back plate. At that point I was focused on Sabrina." He frowned. "I'm sorry I don't have more information for you."

"You have nothing to be sorry for," Joy said. "You were so helpful yesterday—and so helpful now. We really appreciate everything you've done. And to have you still helping Sabrina is a blessing."

"Yes," Sabrina added. "Thank you."

Lance grinned and then said to Joy, "Believe me, if I remember anything more, I'll let you know." He turned to Sabrina. "And I sincerely hope I won't see you in here again. I hope your CT scan will be good and you'll be released."

"I hope so too," Sabrina said.

After Lance left, Joy sat down by Sabrina's bed. "Did you let Rob know you had the CT scan?"

"Not yet." She took out her phone. "But I will."

Sabrina texted back and forth for a few minutes and then said, "They're still at the birthday party. He'll text when they start home so you can meet them there."

"Do you want me to stay?" Joy asked. "Or do you want to rest?"

"Would you stay while I rest?" Sabrina asked. "I'd like you to be here if the doctor comes in before Rob gets back."

"Yes," Joy said. "Of course."

Sabrina closed her eyes, and soon her breathing slowed. Joy pulled out her phone and texted Ashley. DID YOU FIND HANNAH'S WATER BOTTLE YESTERDAY? IT DROPPED TO THE FLOOR WHEN SHE FAINTED.

A text came back a few minutes later. NO. IT'S NOT HERE.

DID REBEKAH GET THE SEARCH WARRANT YET? WOULD SHE HAVE TAKEN IT?

NO SEARCH WARRANT. MAYBE SHE DECIDED AGAINST IT SINCE THERE'S NO EVIDENCE THAT HANNAH WAS POISONED IN THE SHOP.

Maybe. Or perhaps Rebekah was too busy with the other cases she was working on. Maybe she'd acquire the search warrant later in the day.

Joy typed in another text. WHAT ABOUT THE NEW REP WITH SUN BEAUTY SUPPLY? DO YOU THINK IT WAS COINCIDENTAL THAT HE SHOWED UP AT THE SHOP WHEN HE DID? HE LOOKED FAMILIAR TO ME.

It was a few minutes until Ashley texted back—Joy guessed she'd been waiting on a client. I'VE NEVER SEEN HIM BEFORE, BUT THE TURNOVER FOR REPS IS PRETTY HIGH.

CAN YOU CONTACT THE COMPANY AND ASK ABOUT THE LATEST REP? NAME, DESCRIPTION, ETC.

YEAH. I'LL CHECK IN WITH THE SUPERVISOR FOR OUR AREA.

Joy went back to researching Ernest Crane. On the fourth page, she found a short article from 1987. A Charles Ernest Crane, proprietor of an auto body shop located in the Crane Building, was arrested on June 10 for theft. Joy googled *sentencing for Charles Ernest Crane* but didn't find anything—at first. Finally, she found a short notice from 1987 that he'd been sentenced for six years. Then an arrest from 1999 for burglary, but she couldn't find a sentencing from that case.

She texted Evelyn. Do you know anything about Charles Ernest Crane? Any trouble he was involved in, specifically?

It's a long story, Evelyn texted back. And I'm at work right now.

Are you busy? Joy responded. I'm at the hospital. With Sabrina.

It's as slow as molasses, came Evelyn's response. I'll be right up.

Joy waited for Evelyn in the fourth-floor waiting room, where she could watch for the doctor. She stood when she saw Evelyn.

"How is Sabrina?" Evelyn asked as she approached.

"All right. Waiting on the results from her CT scan. If the doctor arrives, I'll need to go back to the room."

"Of course," Evelyn said.

Joy took her notebook from her purse. "I googled Ernest Crane. Any chance he's Charles Ernest Crane?"

Evelyn tilted her head. "Probably. His grandfather's name was Charles."

"I came across an article that he was charged with theft in 1987 and then another article about a burglary conviction in 1999."

"I don't know if I ever knew about the 1999 conviction," Evelyn said. "But I remember the 1987 charge."

"I found that he was sentenced to six years."

"That sounds right. I remember it being at least five."

"And he's Sassie's cousin?"

Evelyn nodded. "Her first cousin. Their fathers were brothers. She and Ernest grew up together and were close, until he opened a chop shop in the warehouse side of the Crane building, or at least he was convicted of theft that had to do with the auto shop."

"Wow. Do you think they stayed in touch all these years?"

Evelyn shook her head. "I guess there were a lot of hard feelings on Ernest's part toward Sassie, plus I think Sassie was mortified by the entire ordeal. A lot of people thought Sassie was involved. Then their grandfather left the Crane House and the Crane Building to Sassie."

"Why not to his sons?"

"Sassie's father died in Vietnam," Evelyn said.

Joy exhaled slowly. Poor Sassie. "What happened to Ernest's father?"

"He died in a drunk driving accident."

"How horrible."

"Yes. He hit another car—a young woman, who was badly injured. He died at the scene of the crash."

"He was at fault?"

"He was," Evelyn said. "He had a drinking problem that everyone knew about. Life got a lot harder for Ernest after his father died, but he had a good head for business, and it seemed, with his grandfather's help, that he was going to do all right."

Joy scribbled some notes. "Anything else you can think of to tell me?"

"No, but I'll text if something comes to mind."

"Do you know of anyone who may have kept in touch with Ernest?"

"Besides Sassie, Hannah, or Parker?"

"Yes," Joy answered.

"I don't. And I'd be surprised if any of them did. There were a lot of hard feelings by the time he was sentenced."

"Interesting." Joy closed her notebook. "Let me know if you think of anything or see anyone."

After thanking Evelyn, Joy hurried back down the hall and into Sabrina's room. A moment later, the neurosurgeon—Dr. Reynolds—arrived.

Joy met Sabrina's gaze with a smile. On the outside, she hoped she appeared calm and collected. On the inside, her nerves were fraying.

"I have the results of the CT scan," Dr. Reynolds said. "The pressure is building in your brain, and we may need to operate within the next day or so. I can't say for sure, but I can't let you go home. Is your husband around?"

"No," Sabrina said. "He's with our girls."

"Can he join us? I imagine he has some questions for me. I can come back in about forty-five minutes."

With tears in her eyes, Sabrina turned to Joy. "Rob and the girls just got home. Could you call Auntie Hope and ask her to go to our house and watch the girls? And then call Rob and ask him to get up here as quickly as possible so he can speak with the doctor?"

"Yes." As Joy dialed Hope, she said to Sabrina, "Once Rob arrives, I can go stay with the girls."

"No," Sabrina said. "I want you here too. I need both you and Rob to listen to what the doctor has to say."

Chapter Seven

Rob was at the hospital within thirty minutes, and the doctor was back in the room in forty with the CT scan. He pointed out where Sabrina's brain was swelling. "The blood is continuing to pool and put pressure on the brain." He looked at Sabrina. "How are your pain levels?"

"A little worse today."

"All right. I'll increase your meds." He glanced at Rob and then Joy and then back at Sabrina. "There's still a chance that the blood will stop pooling and the swelling will go down. We'll do another CT scan in the morning." He clasped his hands together. "Any questions?"

Rob inhaled and seemed ready to ask something. Joy wondered if he should speak with the doctor in private. Rob exhaled. "So if it comes to surgery, you'd do the craniotomy?"

"Yes," Dr. Reynolds answered. "It's a surgery I've done many times before with great success." He looked directly at Rob. "Any more questions?"

Rob shook his head.

After the doctor left, Joy said, "I'll let you two have some time together. I'll go home and stay with the girls."

"We'll call and give them an update and tell them not to worry," Sabrina said. "And you should take some time for yourself. Auntie

Hope will be disappointed if she has to leave so soon. Stop and get a cup of coffee. Take a couple of deep breaths."

Joy bent down and kissed Sabrina on the cheek, touched that her daughter was thinking of her when facing such uncertainty. Joy felt as if she was teetering on the verge of uncertainty, on her wobbly inner knees. But she couldn't give in to it. She had to be strong for Sabrina and her family.

She was also tempted to dwell on Wilson's death—but she couldn't do that either. She wouldn't go there, not now.

She gave Sabrina a hug and then Rob one too. After telling them goodbye, Joy stepped out into the hall and saw Parker Hollingsworth walking toward her. "Are you Joy Atkins?"

"Yes, I am."

Parker crossed his arms. "I need to speak with you."

She pointed to the sitting area. "That's fine, but I'd rather do it away from my daughter's room."

Parker glanced at the door. "Your daughter is in the hospital?"

Joy led the way down the hall. "Yes. She was injured in a hit-and-run accident yesterday, near the Crane Building."

He took a step backward. "Have they caught the driver?"

"No," Joy answered. "There's not even a lead yet."

"Is your daughter going to be all right?"

"Yes," Joy replied, not wanting to discuss Sabrina with the man. She sat down in a chair and motioned to the one across from her. "What can I help you with?"

"Hannah said you were at Sassie's with her when she lost consciousness."

"I was."

"Did you notice anything odd? Especially as far as Sassie's behavior? Did you see her mix anything weird into Hannah's hair dye?"

"No." Joy shook her head firmly.

"How about after Hannah lost consciousness? How did Sassie react then?"

"She seemed very concerned."

"The other stylist said Sassie was paralyzed. That you were the one who helped Hannah."

Joy met Parker's gaze. "Sassie was very upset."

"How about Ashley? How did she respond?"

"She was upset too—she called 911."

"Anything else you can tell me that might help me figure out what went wrong yesterday?"

"No," Joy said. "It was my first hair appointment with Sassie, so I don't have anything to compare it to. But nothing seemed unusual. Hannah had canceled her appointment, and Sassie gave it to me—but then Hannah showed up, so that was a little awkward."

"Why did she cancel her appointment?"

"You didn't know?"

Parker shook his head.

"You should ask her." Joy stood. "I need to get going."

"Do you have another minute?" Parker asked. "Would you come down to Hannah's room with me?"

Joy pursed her lips.

He exhaled slowly. "Please? In case Hannah has any questions for you."

"All right." Joy followed him down the hall into Hannah's room.

"Sweetie," Parker said, "I'm wondering if you have any questions for Joy about what you don't remember from yesterday."

Hannah appeared puzzled but said, "Hello again, Joy." She looked up at Parker. "I don't have any questions."

"Joy said you canceled your appointment with Sassie yesterday and then showed up anyway," Parker said. "Why did you cancel?"

"Oh, I was feeling overwhelmed in the morning. Like I had too much to do. But by afternoon, I felt better."

Parker stepped to the side of the bed and took her hand. "You were feeling overwhelmed because of me?"

Hannah rolled her shoulders. "It was everything."

Parker turned to Joy. "I've been having some health problems—Hannah has been worried."

That fit with Hannah telling Sassie that Parker was acting strange that morning and that he had a doctor's appointment the next Wednesday. "I'm sorry to hear you're having health problems," Joy said. "And that your family now has Hannah's health to be concerned about too."

"I'm hoping that once we can figure out who poisoned Hannah and with what, she can be on the road to recovery."

"What did the toxicology report indicate?" Joy asked. "Did it show she was poisoned?"

"The preliminary tests were inconclusive. We're hiring another lab to run the tests."

"What are the possibilities of being poisoned by hair dye?" Joy asked.

"It depends on what Sassie used," Parker answered. "I have a chemist friend I've consulted with, and he says it's possible. Sassie uses a special henna formula on Hannah—Sassie's own formula—and my friend said she could have mixed something into it that would accumulate over time and could have poisoned Hannah."

"Which means it would have been a coincidence that Hannah collapsed yesterday at the salon, right?" Joy asked. "If it'd been accumulating over time, it could have happened anywhere."

"Most likely."

"Parker," Hannah said, "Sassie would never poison me."

He patted her leg. "I know, I know. I can't believe it either. But what if she did? Or maybe Ashley did."

"You're being paranoid," Hannah said.

Parker muttered, "I have reasons to be paranoid."

"Why?" Hannah asked. "What reason do you have?"

Parker sighed. "We have a long history with Sassie."

Hannah shook her head. "That was long ago. It has nothing to do with me collapsing in Sassie's shop. It appears I have some sort of kidney condition. We need to concentrate on that—and on Lindsay and on your health." Hannah turned to Joy. "Thank you for humoring Parker, but I know you have worries of your own. We don't want to keep you."

Joy nodded. "I do need to go. I hope you'll be feeling better soon, Hannah." She directed her gaze to Parker, who was now staring at his wife's bed. "Nice to meet you."

"Nice to meet you." He glanced up and then redirected his gaze back to Hannah.

As Joy left Hannah's room, she heard a sob. She couldn't help but look back, expecting to see Parker comforting Hannah. But it was the other way around. She was comforting him.

Joy sat back down in the waiting room, in the same chair she'd used while speaking with Parker, and took out her phone. She had questions. Hopefully Evelyn and Anne could answer them.

Could I crash your coffee date?

Of course, Anne texted back.

I'm on my way, Evelyn texted. See both of you in the Grove.

Ten minutes later the three women sat at a table in the far corner. It was warm, but the privacy of the tree-filled, outdoor courtyard tucked between the hospital buildings was welcome. The pink hibiscus were in bloom, as well as the very first blossoms of the Rose of Sharon bushes.

After Joy gave them an update on Sabrina, she said in a low voice, even though nobody else was in the Grove, "Have you two heard any chatter about Sassie Crane or the Hollingsworths?"

"James said Parker has been trying to buy the Crane Building," Evelyn said.

Joy remembered Parker accusing Sassie of trying to stop him and Sassie telling him it wasn't for sale the evening before. "Is it common knowledge that Parker wants to buy the building? Or do only a few select people know, including college professors?"

Evelyn laughed. "James plays tennis with another developer. Every developer in town would like that property, but if Sassie was going to sell, it would only be to Parker."

"I've heard some chatter." Anne leaned back in her chair, her hands wrapped around her iced coffee. "While running errands, I bumped into a volunteer who told me that Sassie tried to murder Hannah Hollingsworth by poisoning her."

Joy winced.

Evelyn rolled her eyes.

"The volunteer said Sassie mixed up a special batch of hair dye to 'do the dirty deed.'" Anne made air quotes with her fingers.

"How could hair dye poison someone so quickly?" Evelyn asked.

"I wondered that too," Joy said. "But Parker is speculating that Sassie was poisoning Hannah over a long period of time and it was coincidental that she collapsed in the salon. He said the lab results were 'inconclusive' as far as what poison was used, but he's hiring another lab. The tests did show that Hannah has some sort of kidney condition, which could indicate poisoning." She turned to Anne. "Did the volunteer say who she heard the accusation against Sassie from?"

Anne nodded. "From her cousin, who heard it from a friend who heard it from a neighbor."

"Any idea where the neighbor lives?"

Anne nodded again. "On Sullivan's Island, same as Parker and Hannah, although not next door."

Joy's eyebrows shot up. "Sullivan's Island?"

"Uh-huh. The Hollingsworths live in a gorgeous house with a pool in back and the Atlantic in front."

It sounded gorgeous. The island was just north of the Bay. "So maybe the volunteer didn't hear it directly from Parker, but maybe from someone who'd spoken with him," Joy said.

"Most likely," Anne answered.

"And anyone who lives on Sullivan's Island who talks about this is going to be believed, right? They'd be considered credible."

"Of course," Evelyn said. "As would Parker. He might be a big talker, but he's well respected. If he says Sassie poisoned Hannah, people are going to believe it. The Hollingsworths have been close to Sassie all these years. No one would suspect that Parker doesn't have evidence to back up his claim."

Anne placed her hand flat on the tabletop. "Any chance Parker has enough reason or any evidence to accuse Sassie?"

"I guess it's plausible," Joy answered. "If he has evidence though, even motive, I hope he's turned it over to Rebekah."

"Has Rebekah said anything?"

Joy shook her head. "She wouldn't say anything to me, or to Sassie, at this point in the investigation. But Rebekah's busy with other cases. She said she was going to get a search warrant for Sassie's salon last night but hasn't yet. And it's been open all day."

"Yikes," Evelyn said. "So if there was evidence there it might be destroyed by now?"

"Perhaps." Joy glanced from Evelyn to Anne and back to Evelyn. "So tell me about Parker and Hannah Hollingsworth."

"They were two years behind me in school," Evelyn said. "He was the second-string varsity quarterback as a sophomore and then ended up first string after the senior quarterback broke his leg. She was a cheerleader. So was Sassie. They were all close, popular, and well known."

"Were they friends with Sassie's cousin too?" Joy asked.

"They were," Evelyn said. "I was thinking about that after we talked earlier. Ernest was part of their group." She chuckled. "Early in high school they called themselves the Dream Team. This was long before the basketball dream teams. I'm not sure where they got the idea. But it was catchy. And it wasn't just because the boys played football. They all—including Sassie and Hannah—had high aspirations, or so it seemed. I doubt Parker would have kept in touch with Ernest through the years." Evelyn took a sip of her coffee. "There was another young man in that group—Riley something. He played football too although he wasn't the standout that the other two were. I didn't know him."

"Is he still in the Charleston area?" Joy asked.

"I don't know." Evelyn shrugged.

Joy jumped to her next thought. "When Sassie ducked into the gift shop yesterday morning, she said she'd been visiting an 'old friend.' Any idea who that might have been?"

Evelyn shook her head.

"Her cousin?"

Evelyn shrugged again. "Not if he was the person trailing her through the lobby."

"True." Joy thought for a moment and then asked, "You sure you can't remember Riley's last name?"

"I'm sure," Evelyn said. "But I remember something else about him. He ended up in the hospital about the time Ernest was arrested."

Anne leaned forward. "Wow. You remember that from all those years ago?"

Evelyn nodded. "I'd just started working in the records department. It made an impression on me."

Anne put her coffee cup down. "What was wrong with him?"

Evelyn grimaced. "I'm afraid to say. In fact, I'm wondering if I can trust my memory."

"What do you remember?" Joy asked.

"That he was poisoned."

Chapter Eight

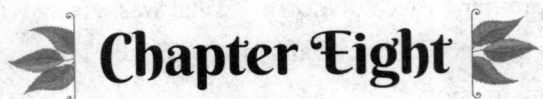

AFTER ANNE LEFT TO GO home and Evelyn went back to work, Joy headed to the Crane Building to check in with Ashley. As she approached, three forensic team members from the Charleston PD climbed into a white van. Then Rebekah stepped out the door, followed by Ashley.

"So we can get back to business?" Joy heard Ashley ask.

"Yes," Rebekah said. "I'll let you know if we have any follow-up questions or need to see anything in the shop again."

Joy took a step back, not wanting to eavesdrop.

Rebekah motioned for her to join them.

"What about the warehouse, where the safe was taken?" Ashley asked Rebekah.

"Detective Lee already went through that with your mother yesterday."

"And no one is going to go through it again?"

Rebekah shook her head. "Not unless something comes up." She lowered her voice. "Did you ever see the safe that was stolen?"

Ashley shook her head.

"Your mother couldn't name anyone else who'd seen it either."

"What about the guys working in the warehouse? Mother said they found it."

"Did she say 'they' found it? Or it was found during the construction process? She told Detective Lee she found it."

"Oh." Ashley pursed her lips together. "Interesting."

Rebekah put her notebook in her pocket. "Let me know if anything comes up. If you think of anything or if your mother does. Or if Parker or Hannah Hollingsworth say anything more to you."

"I will," Ashley said.

As Rebekah took a step toward her car, Joy asked, "Any progress on finding out who hit Sabrina?"

Rebekah shook her head. "I've requested security film from the hospital, but I'm not sure it will show the intersection. I've checked with the other businesses on the street that have cameras, but none are aimed at the intersection."

"How about information about the vehicle, based on the description?"

Rebekah sighed. "A black SUV with no identifying info—no bumper stickers, not even a license plate number."

"So you're saying you don't feel hopeful you'll find the vehicle or the driver?"

"No, that's not what I'm saying. What I am saying is that we don't have any identifying information at this time." She took another step toward her car. "Goodbye, ladies. Give me a call if anything comes up."

"All right," Joy said. "Goodbye."

Ashley waved, half-heartedly, and then turned to the shop's entrance. Joy followed her.

"Do you have any clients?" Joy asked.

Ashley shook her head. "I had to send our stylists and estheticians home once Rebekah called to say she had a warrant. I rescheduled all of the appointments." Ashley stepped to the desk and patted the appointment book. "We're going to have a crazy day on Monday."

Joy knew they would, starting with her six thirty A.M. haircut. "Did the forensic team find anything?"

"They wanted the empty dye bottles Mother used, both for Hannah and you, but the cleaners came last night."

"Are they out in the dumpster?"

Ashley shook her head. "It was picked up this morning."

"How about the supply of henna your mother uses for Hannah's special formula, for your mother's trademark dye?"

Ashley frowned. "I've never actually seen any henna here."

"How odd."

"Yeah," Ashley said. "I don't understand all of that. All I know is that I've never seen henna in the shop."

"Interesting," Joy said. "Has Hannah's water bottle shown up?"

Ashley shook her head. "Any chance one of the EMTs picked it up and put it in her bag?"

"I don't think so." Joy pointed to the area where the chairs were. "Mind if I look?"

"No," Ashley said. "But I doubt you'll find anything the rest of us missed."

Joy shrugged. "Probably not."

She walked to the chair Hannah had been sitting in, climbed up into it, and then imagined dropping a metal bottle. Where would it roll? There was a counter across the way with a high baseboard. Nothing had wedged under it. Joy scooted out of the chair and walked across the room then opened the cabinet above where the bottle might have landed. Clean towels were stacked inside. Joy got down on her knees and peered inside. Nothing.

Joy stood. "I can't remember what happened to her book either. I know it hit the floor, but I can't remember if anyone picked it up or not."

"Things were pretty chaotic," Ashley said. "There was a lot going on."

Joy agreed. "Do you have any idea who your mother would have been visiting yesterday morning at the hospital?"

"She was visiting someone?"

Joy nodded. "She said it was an old friend."

"I don't know of anyone who's sick."

"It was right after I opened, just after eight."

"We don't unlock the door until nine on Fridays, so that would have been before we opened." Ashley shook her head. "Mother goes through phases of being secretive. I mean, she's been mysterious her whole life. But sometimes more so than others."

"In what ways?"

"Well, the biggest secret she's kept is who my father is. She's never told me."

"Really? No clue at all?"

Ashley shook her head. "It really bothered me in my teens and early twenties, but I've come to accept that she'll never tell me. He's not listed on my birth certificate. And I'm pretty sure she swore Parker and Hannah to secrecy—they said they don't know, but I don't really believe them."

"What other secrets has she kept?"

"Oh, little things," Ashley said. "Like why she decided to start the construction project for the expanded spa immediately after Barry died without mentioning her idea at all to me before she started." Ashley rubbed the back of her neck. "I get it. It's her life. Her business. But her lack of transparency has been hard for me. I love my mother, but she's never been a normal kind of mother. Not like you are to Sabrina."

Joy didn't respond.

"I mean, I know she loves me." Ashley's eyes grew watery. "She provided a good home for me. Helped me figure out how to pay for college. And now she's taken me into the business and is letting me live in the apartment above the shop for less rent than she could get from someone else. In time, I'll be able to pay off the debt from Barry's business—so she *is* helping me. But nothing has ever felt simple with her. She's always been a little standoffish. She's never been warm and fuzzy like other mothers."

"There are all sorts of different styles of mothers."

Ashley smiled. "I know. Same with daughters. I'm nothing but grateful to my mother for all she's done for me. But I get a little jealous when I hear about Sabrina's childhood. A mom who was always around. A devoted father."

Wilson had been absolutely devoted. Joy's heart ached for Ashley, that she didn't have that support and didn't even know who her father was.

Joy cleared her throat. "I have one more question. Did you hear back from the hair product company about the new sales rep?"

"Yes." Ashley held up her phone. "The district manager texted me back. She said they don't have a new rep—just their old one. Some woman named Violet."

Joy wrinkled her nose. "How odd."

"I know, right?" Ashley crossed her arms over her chest. "There's all sorts of strange things going on around here."

When Joy arrived at Sabrina's house, Hope and the girls were in the backyard. Mallory was running through bubbles, generated by the machine Joy had bought the girls for Easter. Eloise sat in a chair on the patio sipping lemonade. And Hope was weeding in the far flower bed.

"Who's hungry?" Joy asked as she stepped out the patio door, holding up a bag filled with dinner from Kickin' Carryout.

"I am!" Mallory yelled.

Eloise shaded her eyes with her free hand. "How's Mom?"

"All right." Joy placed the bag on the table. "She misses you."

"Can we go see her?"

"You'll need to ask your dad." Joy had hoped Sabrina would be out of the hospital by now, but it would be good if the girls could see her if she wasn't going to be discharged tomorrow. It would ease their worries. Maybe after church, they could go up to the hospital.

"Come wash your hands," Joy told the girls. "And then we'll eat."

Eloise headed to the door while Mallory started running through the bubbles again.

"Come on, Mallory." Hope shut off the machine. "Let's go wash up."

"Thank you," Joy said to Hope as she led Mallory to the door.

Joy put out the boxes of chicken nuggets for the girls, fries for all of them, and chicken sandwiches for Hope and herself. Then she pulled out the paper plates and napkins.

After Hope and the girls sat down, Joy led the four of them in a prayer, thanking the Lord for the food and asking for healing for Sabrina, and then she headed into the kitchen for lemonade for Mallory and sweet tea for Hope and herself. When she returned, everyone sat at the table with a plate in front of them.

"What a lovely evening." Joy passed the boxes of chicken nuggets and some fries to the girls.

Hope opened a ketchup packet and passed it to Eloise. "It's great to spend it with all of you."

Joy handed Hope her sandwich and fries. "Thank you for helping out."

"No problem," Hope said. "Thank you for sharing your family with me."

Joy's eyes filled with tears. "It's not sharing. It's family. We need you."

Hope put her arm around Joy and squeezed.

"Aww," Eloise said. "You two are so cute."

"We're sisters," Hope said. "We're here for each other."

Mallory put her arm around Eloise and faked a grin. They all laughed, including Eloise.

After they finished supper, Hope helped Joy clean up. As Joy loaded the dishes into the dishwasher, the girls settled down in the family room to watch a show.

"How is Hannah Hollingsworth?" Hope lowered her voice. "Does Parker still think she was poisoned?"

Joy nodded. "She seems to be doing all right, but she's still in the hospital."

A few minutes later, Hope told Joy and the girls goodbye. After the girls' show was over, Joy read to Mallory while Eloise took a shower and then Joy ran Mallory's bath. By the time the girls were ready for bed, Rob arrived home.

"How's Mommy?" Eloise asked.

He wrapped his arm around her. "The same."

Eloise leaned against him.

Fifteen minutes later, Joy arrived home, exhausted, to find a bouquet of pale pink and white peonies on her porch, delivered by a florist. Her name was on the envelope.

She picked up the bouquet, unlocked her front door, and headed to her kitchen, where she put the flowers on the table.

She pulled the card from the envelope. It was from Roger Gaylord. He was a wealthy benefactor for the hospital and a pillar of Charleston society. The card read, *Anne told me about Sabrina's accident. Please know she—and you—are in my prayers. Warmly, Roger*

She'd told him recently that she hoped to add peonies to her flower garden.

Her phone dinged. It was a text from Sabrina. Roger sent me the most beautiful bouquet of peonies. So sweet of him.

A sensation of warmth swept through Joy. She responded to Sabrina and then drafted a text to Roger. Thank you so much for the flowers for both Sabrina and me. We truly appreciate your prayers. She hit send. He immediately texted back. I was so sorry to hear about the accident. What do you need? Please let me know. She smiled as she texted him back. She assured him their needs were currently being met, but she'd let him know if they needed additional help.

Her friendship with Roger was growing, but she hadn't texted him about Sabrina. She wasn't sure why—she knew he'd want to know. She was glad Anne had told him. God only knew how their relationship would turn out—but he was a good man, and she was thankful for him.

She centered the flowers on the table and then headed out the back door to the flowers she was growing. A drip irrigation system watered most of her plants, but she hadn't extended the system to her hanging baskets. After watering them, she headed back into the house and poured herself a glass of ice water with a sprig of mint and sat down on the couch with her laptop. She logged onto the South Carolina archives website. She typed in *Sassie Crane* but nothing appeared, not even a birth certificate. It dawned on Joy that Sassie was probably a nickname. But for what?

She googled "Sassie Crane." A page of links appeared. First was the salon website. Then an article about the Charleston Chamber of Commerce, with Sassie included. Then a fundraiser for foster children, with donations from Sassie listed. There were more links about fundraisers and charity events. No other name besides "Sassie" showed up.

Next she googled *Bay Development, Charleston, SC*. A photo of Parker popped up and then one of him with Hannah at a gala. Parker was dressed in a tuxedo, and Hannah was wearing a stunning strapless black gown. The next photo was of Parker and three men playing golf. Joy searched for a website and then clicked on what she found.

The text on the home page read: *Bay Development is a real estate investment and development company. We maximize returns for our investors through discovering and developing a wide variety of properties and projects.*

Following were pictures of recent projects. An executive center. A business park. A hotel in the suburbs. An apartment complex. A high-rise condo building north of Charleston with the beach in the background.

Parker was listed as a managing partner in the firm, and Hannah was listed as the director of accounting. Joy hadn't realized Hannah worked for the company at all.

Next, she clicked on an article about the company selling a property in North Charleston the year before without developing it. There was a short court notice about Bay Development paying a fine for a missing permit and then an article that included an interview with Parker in which he declared that Charleston needed more condos as well as more apartments. "I'd love to build a mix of high-end and low-income condos in the same building," Parker said to the reporter. "There are several properties we're looking at, all in historic neighborhoods, to build condominiums and help alleviate the housing shortage in the city."

High-end and low-income condos. Charleston certainly needed additional housing. More and more people were moving to the area, pushing up the price of real estate and forcing people out who had lived in the city for years but could no longer afford to buy or even rent. It would be nice if Parker aimed to help resolve that. But surely he wasn't trying to buy the historic Crane Building to tear it down for condos. That would be a crime against the city—and against the

Crane family as well. Maybe he hoped to raise the roof. Of course, no matter what he planned to do, he'd have to have the project approved by the city's Board of Architectural Review. But Joy guessed Parker had had many such projects approved through the years.

The next morning while Rob returned to the hospital, Joy took Eloise and Mallory to Saint Jude's. The church was a hundred and fifty years old, built from stucco, and had a traditional high steeple. The front doors were painted red and always felt like a transition from the worries of the world into the hope of one's faith.

After the opening hymn, Reverend Neal led the welcoming prayer. He included Sabrina in his prayer for the ill. Then, when the children gathered around the pulpit, the kids' pastor spoke of Jesus healing the sick and prayed for Sabrina too. As Mallory and Eloise traipsed out of the sanctuary to children's church, Mallory gave Joy a thumbs-up. Joy smiled back with a lump in her throat and then settled in for the sermon. However, it was hard for her to concentrate as her thoughts kept falling to Sabrina and the events of the past several days.

After church was over, Joy drove the girls to the hospital. Rob met them in the cafeteria for lunch—macaroni and cheese for Eloise, pepperoni pizza for Mallory, a burger for Rob, and a chopped salad for Joy. Once everyone was done eating, as they readied their trays, Rob said, "Guess what?"

"What?" Mallory grinned.

"You two get to go see Mommy now."

Eloise clapped her hands together in delight. "Finally!"

Mallory, however, grew quiet.

"What's wrong, baby?" Rob asked.

"Is Mommy the same as she was—you know—before?"

"Of course," Rob said.

After they bussed their table, the four headed through the lobby to the elevators. Eloise reached for Joy's hand and slowed down while Mallory marched past Rob and hit the up button. Eloise continued to hold Joy's hand but slowed as they neared the elevator.

Joy bent her head to Eloise. "Is something wrong?"

Eloise shook her head.

When they reached the fourth floor, Mallory bolted out of the elevator, asking, "Which way?"

"To the right," Rob said. "Room 417."

As Joy stepped off the elevator, Eloise's hand still in hers, she saw Sassie stepping into a room at the end of the hall. It wasn't Hannah's room, unless she'd been moved.

Mallory marched ahead with Rob following her closely. But Eloise was practically dragging her feet now. Joy stopped and stooped down, still clutching Eloise's hand and putting her free arm around her granddaughter's shoulder. "Are you anxious about seeing your mom?"

Eloise shrugged, but tears sprang into her eyes.

"It's normal to feel nervous in a hospital." Joy realized she and Rob should have prepared the girls more. "Your mom will be in the hospital bed. The TV will be off, and the window shades drawn because it's not good for her to see bright or flashing lights right now. She'll be so happy to see you. There are two chairs in the room. You can sit on one of those. Or stand. Or sit on the edge of Mommy's bed. No matter what you're feeling, it's normal. If you need anything from your dad or from me, make sure and let us know."

"Okay," Eloise whispered.

"Do you have any questions?"

"Is it my fault Mommy is hurt?"

"Eloise, why would you think that?"

"I didn't want her to leave that day. I kept asking her questions. I kept asking her not to leave. Finally she said she was going to be late if she didn't get out the door. If I'd let her go sooner, she wouldn't have been hit."

"No, it's not your fault. Not at all. It's the fault of the person who hit her." Joy pulled her close. "Do you understand it's not your fault?"

Eloise nodded.

"Do you have any other questions?"

Eloise shook her head.

"Make sure if you do, to ask me or your dad or your mom," Joy said. "All of us want you to be as comfortable as possible." Joy squeezed Eloise's hand. "Ready?"

Eloise squeezed her hand back and smiled.

Rob stuck his head out the door. "Everything all right?"

Joy smiled at him.

Rob beckoned to Eloise. "Mommy's asking for you."

Eloise finally picked up her pace.

When they stepped into the room, Sabrina beamed. "There you are." She patted the side of the bed. "Come sit with us, El."

Mallory was already on one side of the bed. Joy walked with Eloise to the other and then lifted her up. Sabrina gave Eloise a hug and then patted Mallory's hand. "I've been missing both of you so much. I'm so glad you came up to see me."

"We've been worried about you," Eloise said.

Mallory added, "And we've been missing you."

Rob sat at the end of the bed, a grin on his face. Joy decided to leave the family alone for a few minutes. She slipped out the door and across the hall to Hannah's room. The door was open, providing a view of Hannah in the bed.

"Hello," Joy said.

"Come in."

Joy stepped into the room. Hannah was by herself, sitting up in bed. "How are you feeling?"

"Much better." Hannah smiled. "I'm going home this afternoon. Hopefully soon."

"That's wonderful. Any new results as far as your tests?"

Hannah shook her head. "I definitely have kidney damage and have an appointment with a nephrologist on Tuesday. They're not sure if the damage is recent or not. I've had some ongoing symptoms that I didn't recognize—fatigue, trouble sleeping, and itchy skin—but not for long."

"I'm sorry about the kidney damage—and I'm glad you have an appointment so soon."

Hannah nodded in agreement.

"I was thinking about something yesterday," Joy said. "About your water bottle."

"My what?"

"The water bottle you had with you on Friday. Did you end up with it?"

"I think it's in my bag," Hannah said.

"Oh, that's good to hear." Joy glanced around. "What about your book?"

"It's probably in my bag too," Hannah said. "Parker took it home so I wouldn't have to keep track of it here."

Joy smiled.

Hannah patted her hair. "I need to get in to see Sassie for a cut. And probably a redo on my color too."

"Your hair looks great, considering."

Hannah grinned. "Yours too. But you got your color and cut."

"Oh, I didn't get a cut yet," Joy said. "I'm getting that done tomorrow."

Hannah's face fell. "Sassie is cutting your hair tomorrow?"

"At six thirty in the morning." Joy covered her mouth as she yawned.

"Well, I don't want an appointment that early, but I wish she'd return my texts and schedule something this week. She's been acting really strange."

"Has she been up to see you?"

"No." Hannah's face reddened. "I have no idea what's going on with her. Maybe Parker's right. Maybe Sassie did poison me."

Joy grimaced. "I didn't mean to upset you."

Hannah frowned. "Sassie is the one who's upset me. You've been nothing but kind." Then she yawned and said, "I think I'll rest until I'm discharged."

"All right," Joy said. "Please take care."

Hannah gave Joy a little wave.

As Joy left the room, she glanced down the hall toward the room Sassie had stepped into. No one was in sight. Then she turned to Sabrina's room. At the end of the hall, stepping into the elevator, was Sassie.

Joy hid behind Hannah's half-open door, not wanting Sassie to see her. A minute later, Joy stepped back to the middle of the hall and stared at the closed elevator for a moment. She took a step toward Sabrina's room, until a shuffle behind her drew her attention. She looked over her shoulder. A thin man with a gaunt face, wearing a hospital gown, bathrobe, slippers, and a cowboy hat leaned on a cane carved out of wood with a saddle for the handle. He stood in the doorway of the room Sassie had slipped into earlier. He appeared to be in his late sixties or so, but she guessed he was ill, so perhaps that had aged him.

He started to shuffle toward her.

"Good afternoon," Joy said.

"Good afternoon to you." He tipped his hat with his free hand. He didn't speak with a Texas accent—or even a Southern one—as she expected him to. In fact, she didn't recognize his accent at all.

Joy smiled. "I thought by your hat you might be from Texas, but by your accent I'd say no."

He grinned. "Montana," he said. "Although I grew up down here. I don't know when it happened, but somewhere along the way, I lost my accent." He grinned. "I also lost my manners. I know I shouldn't be wearing my hat indoors, but…" He shrugged. "It makes me feel a little bit better about being in here."

Joy gave him a sympathetic smile. "What are you doing back in Charleston?"

"I came to visit an old friend." He gripped his cane tighter. "Before it's too late—but then I ended up in here."

Joy felt a pang of sympathy for the man. "I'm sorry."

"It's all right," he said. "The Lord knows the number of my days. I'm just glad I made it home. I didn't expect to spend my time in the hospital. I collapsed a couple of days ago. I thought I had time to take care of some business, but we'll see if the Lord allows me to or not."

He tipped his hat again and then said, "I'm afraid I don't have as much energy as I thought. Excuse me, I'm going to go rest."

"Do you need help?" Joy asked.

"No, ma'am," he said. "Have a good afternoon."

"You too." As Joy walked to Sabrina's room, she wished she'd asked the man's name. He must be the old friend Sassie had visited Friday morning before she ducked into the gift shop—and the one she continued to visit.

Chapter Nine

A HALF HOUR LATER, BACK in Sabrina's room, Joy said she'd take the girls home.

"Rob, why don't you take them home?" Sabrina sighed. "I should rest."

Joy stepped to Sabrina's side while Rob collected the girls and whispered, "Are you feeling okay?"

Sabrina nodded. "Mostly," she whispered back. "I'm going to get my pain meds and sleep."

Rob put his arms around the girls' shoulders. "Tell Mommy goodbye."

"Will we see you tomorrow?" Eloise asked Sabrina.

"I hope to be home tomorrow," Sabrina answered. "You both have sports camp. Daddy will take you. If I get out of the hospital, I'll pick you up. If not, Miss Anne will, and you'll stay with Addie for a little while."

Mallory clapped her hands together.

"If you do stay at Miss Anne's, I need you to behave," Sabrina said to Mallory. "All right?"

Mallory twirled around, her hot-pink dress lifting up in a circle, showing her pink shorts underneath. Then she grinned.

"Mallory," Sabrina said. "Please stop moving."

Mallory sobered instantly. "Sorry."

"Come here," Sabrina said, stretching her hand to her youngest.

Mallory rushed to her mother and took her hand. Sabrina pulled her to the side of the bed.

"I need you to do your best at sports camp, and then if you go home with Addie, listen carefully to Miss Anne."

Mallory sighed and then said, "Okay."

"Say 'yes, ma'am' without the attitude."

Mallory's volume decreased. "Yes, ma'am."

"That's my girl." Sabrina kissed the top of Mallory's head.

Joy told Sabrina goodbye, saying a silent prayer as she kissed her cheek, and then she stood in the hallway with the girls to wait for Rob. As they waited, Ashley stepped off the elevator.

Mallory waved and called out, "Hello!"

Ashley waved back and approached them. "How is Sabrina? Is she up for another visitor?"

"No," Eloise replied before Joy could say anything. "Mommy needs to sleep."

Ashley smiled. "Of course. I'm so glad I saw the three of you before I woke her."

Rob came out, said hello to Ashley, and then told the girls it was time to go.

"Bye, Mimi." Mallory gave her a hug, followed by Eloise.

"Goodbye, girls," Joy said. "I'll see you tomorrow."

After they left, Ashley said, "I want to say hello to Hannah."

"I'll wait for you," Joy said. "I have a question."

Ashley reappeared a minute later. "She's resting too."

As they started for the elevator, a voice called out, "Hello again!"

Joy turned around. The man in the cowboy hat waved at her. Ashley turned too. Joy started toward him, figuring it would be better if she took the walk instead of him.

"I didn't introduce myself before," she said. "I'm Joy Atkins. I manage the gift shop here, and my daughter is a patient on this floor."

"Who's with you?" the man asked.

"I'm Ashley Crane. I'm a friend of Joy's daughter—and of Joy's."

The man grew even paler. "What did you say your name is?"

"Ashley Crane Romero. Crane is my maiden name. Most people in Charleston recognize it."

"No doubt," the man said. "Nice to meet the two of you—Joy and Ashley. I think I'll go rest some more."

"Wait!" Joy realized her voice was too forceful. She lowered it. "You haven't said what your name is."

"I haven't?" He tipped his hat and grinned. "Robert Chorro. But everyone calls me Bob. Some people even call me Cowboy Bob."

Joy raised her hand. "Nice to meet you, Cowboy Bob."

She started walking to the elevator with Ashley right behind her. When they reached it, Ashley said, "That was odd."

"I think that's your mother's 'old friend,'" Joy said as she pushed the lobby button.

"What?"

"I saw her going into his room earlier."

"The cowboy's?"

Joy nodded.

"She doesn't know any cowboys."

"He's from Montana."

"I've never heard her mention anyone in Montana. I've never even heard her mention the state."

As they rode the elevator down to the lobby, Joy said, "You brought up your birth certificate. How was your mother's name listed?"

"Sassie Marie Crane."

"Do you think Sassie is your mother's given name?"

"What do you mean?"

"I assumed 'Sassie' was a nickname."

"I don't think so," Ashley said. "I've never heard—or seen—anything else."

"Interesting," Joy said.

"Why is that interesting?"

"I couldn't find a birth certificate for a Sassie Crane."

"Try Sassie Marie Crane."

"All right. I'll do that as soon as I get home." Joy stopped in the middle of the lobby. "How's the planning coming for your big reopening?"

"Oh, everything's already done except for the day-of stuff. The banners are already made. All the social media posts, emails, and texts are scheduled. All the food and flowers are ordered. The florist and caterer will set up—Mother and I just need to supervise everything."

"Impressive," Joy said.

"That's how Mother's always rolled. Now I just hope Parker's accusations won't sabotage the whole thing."

Joy gave her a sympathetic look.

"Joy! Ashley!" Shirley, wearing a red and purple scarf over her hair, came across the lobby to them. "How is Sabrina doing?"

After Joy gave her an update, Ashley said, "Good to see you, Shirley. I'm going to head on home."

"I'll talk to you soon," Joy said to Ashley. Ashley headed to the exit, and Joy asked Shirley, "What are you doing at the hospital? I thought you had today off."

"I picked up a shift in the emergency room but got to leave early. It's been a rare slow day." She smiled. "I was going to walk to the East Bay Café and get an iced coffee before going home. Want to come with me?"

Joy had planned to go home and do some research but then what? Would she sit around and worry about Sabrina? "Sure," she answered. She could do the research later.

"Any leads on who hit Sabrina?" Shirley asked as they stepped out into the warm Sunday afternoon.

"No," Joy said. "Maybe you could help me think through all of this. Ashley and I tried to get more information from Sassie, but she wasn't very cooperative. And Rebekah and the entire police department seem overwhelmed with other cases."

"I'd love to help," Shirley said as they waited for the walk sign.

As the traffic buzzed by, Joy asked, "Do you have any ideas on how to get Sassie to talk?"

"She's always talkative when we get our pedicures."

"Yes, but what she talks about doesn't have anything to do with her."

Shirley pushed the walk button again. "She's not being helpful when it comes to what happened on Friday?"

"That's right," Joy answered. "She won't even brainstorm about the series of events. In fact, she avoids talking about them."

"Interesting." Shirley squinted across the street, toward the Crane Building. "Is that her speaking with Ashley?"

Joy focused on the two figures. "I believe so."

The walk sign came on and Joy and Shirley started across the street. "Mama caught wind of what happened at the salon and afterward on Friday from a couple of phone conversations with friends," Shirley said. "I told her what I know—from what you told me. I couldn't tell her anything about Sabrina's time in the ER."

"Of course you couldn't," Joy said.

"Anyway, Mama said Sassie has had a lot to deal with in life, and she felt bad that she had to deal with Hannah falling ill in her shop and the safe being stolen."

"So your mother is sympathetic to Sassie?"

"Well, she's more sympathetic to Sabrina and you. But, yes, she cares about Sassie."

Joy did too. But she also felt frustrated with the woman. As they approached Sassie and Ashley, Sassie turned and squinted into the sun. Then she waved. "Oh, hello, Shirley. Hello, Joy."

They waved back, and Joy heard Sassie ask Ashley, "What time is my first appointment tomorrow?"

"You don't have it on your phone?"

Sassie held up her cell. "I'm having problems with it, remember?"

"I know what time your first appointment is," Joy said as she approached. "Six thirty. Me."

Sassie smiled. "That's right. How could I forget? My next one must be at seven thirty."

"And you need to fit Hannah in sometime tomorrow too," Ashley said. "She texted me—again. Because you wouldn't answer any of the twenty-nine hundred texts she's sent you since Friday."

Sassie winced. "I'm not sure when I can fit her in tomorrow."

"I'll look at your schedule and let you know." Ashley crossed her arms.

"We're headed down to East Bay Café," Shirley said to Sassie. "Want to come with us?"

Sassie pursed her lips.

"How about if everyone comes up to my apartment?" Ashley's excited expression seemed a little forced. "I have some cold brew coffee."

"Oh, we don't want to bother you," Joy said.

"It would be fun," Ashley answered. "I don't have people over much."

"All right," Shirley said.

Joy added, "I'm in."

"Mother?"

Sassie wrinkled her nose and said, "All right."

Once Sassie's back was to them, Shirley nudged Joy, who gave her friend a smile. Obviously, Shirley was thinking the same thing she was. Maybe Sassie would give them more information.

They all followed Ashley around the corner and to the gate. Again, Ashley keyed in the code and led the way up the interior stairway to the second floor. The stairs were steep, made of bricks, and well maintained. When they reached the second floor, the stairway continued up to the third floor. Below was the interior courtyard that was filled with palmetto trees, shrubs, and flowers. Ashley turned to the left, toward the corner apartment.

As they walked, Sassie said, "Ashley and I lived here when she was little, until my grandfather passed away. I used to put her to bed, take the baby monitor down with me, and get three more haircuts in from eight until eleven." She exhaled. "I worked so hard back then to make my business and our life together work."

Joy couldn't imagine what it would be like to be a young single mother with a business to grow. She sincerely admired Sassie's work ethic.

Thankfulness for Wilson and what he'd given her and Sabrina overwhelmed her. It wasn't just what he provided through his career. It was also the emotional security he offered, along with his integrity. She couldn't imagine Wilson ever purposefully disappearing from her life, let alone Sabrina's. His daughter was his world—both of their worlds.

Ashley unlocked the door to her apartment and motioned for Sassie to lead the way. Joy and Shirley followed. The apartment was cool and smelled of citrus. A hallway, with a bedroom and bathroom off it, led to an open space with a kitchen and living area, all with interior brick walls. Large windows looked out over the bay. Ashley had furnished the loft in a mix of modern and antique furniture. A velvet gray sectional. An old round cherry table with straight-backed wooden chairs. A linear chandelier with ten bulbs. An old china cabinet filled with blue fluted plates, bowls, cups, and saucers.

A leaded glass bowl of lemons and oranges sat in the middle of the table.

Obviously the citrus smell was from more than the fruit, but the visual was a nice touch. Ashley had created a comfortable home for herself.

"Besides iced coffee, I have sparkling water," Ashley said.

"Water, please," Sassie said.

"I'd love some iced coffee," Shirley said.

"So would I," Joy added.

Ashley's kitchen, which was separated from the living area by a bar, had stainless steel appliances, a gray granite countertop, and gray cupboards. As Ashley stepped to the refrigerator, Sassie sat down at the table. Joy and Shirley joined her.

"Any more problems with your AC?" Sassie asked Ashley.

Ashley shook her head. "Believe me, if I had you'd be the first to know, as both my mother and my landlord."

Joy took her notebook and pen from her purse and placed them on the table, planning to ask Sassie about anything Ashley might forget to bring up.

Sassie stared at the notebook. "That looks serious."

Ashley approached with two beverages.

"I'm hoping to sort through what happened on Friday," Joy said. "What if other people are in danger?"

"No need to overreact," Sassie said. "Hannah wasn't poisoned—she has kidney problems. It was a blessing in disguise that she collapsed. The safe was most likely stolen by some misinformed fool. It was a coincidence—a very unfortunate one—that Sabrina was hit. There's no mystery here. I'm sorry you've been pulled into this. It's a coincidence, I can assure you."

Joy shook her head. "That's not true, Sassie. Even if Hannah wasn't poisoned, you had a safe stolen and I had a daughter injured in a hit-and-run. Those aren't coincidences. At least two crimes have been committed."

"I don't mean to be obtuse," Sassie said. "But Sabrina getting hit was an accident."

"Mother." Ashley sat down at the table with a bottle of sparkling water in her hand. "Don't be so insensitive."

"But it was an accident."

"No, it was a crime. One that could have killed Sabrina. The driver of the SUV ran a red light and then fled a crime scene."

"Sabrina could have died," Shirley said. "She's fortunate that Joy wouldn't let her get up and that she was taken to the hospital immediately."

"You're right," Sassie said. "But I don't think there's any big conspiracy going on."

Joy opened her notebook. "I'm glad you feel that way."

"Why?" Sassie asked.

"Because I have a couple of questions for you."

Sassie hesitated and then said, "All right."

"First," Joy said, "have you heard from your cousin, Ernest Crane, recently?"

"No."

"Have you seen him?"

Sassie didn't answer.

Ashley leaned forward. "Mother."

"Did you see him in the hospital Friday morning?" Joy asked. "In the lobby, when you ran into the gift shop."

"I'm not sure who I saw Friday morning," Sassie answered. "I saw someone who seemed familiar out of the corner of my eye."

"Could it have been Ernest?" Joy asked.

"I haven't seen Ernest in years," Sassie said. "I saw a man who looked more like Ernest's father than Ernest, although Uncle Elmer died when we were in middle school, so I guess he was probably only forty or so. But he always looked old."

"Tell me about the last time you saw Ernest." Joy looked across the table at Sassie. "How long had he been out of prison then?"

Sassie rolled her eyes. "You've obviously done your homework." She sighed. "Ernest had been out of prison a few years last time I saw him. He'd soon be going back, which I could have predicted at the time."

"What did he go back to prison for the second time?"

"Burglary, south of here. He broke into a cabin during the off season and sold some of the stuff he found in there. He was living in it when he was arrested. A few years after that he came around and tried to see me, but I avoided him."

"If the man in the lobby looked like a relative, why didn't you stop to speak to him?" Joy asked.

"Because he bullied me the last time I saw him. Granddaddy had cut Ernest out of his will and was going to leave me both the Crane Building and the Crane House. Ernest wanted me to change Granddaddy's mind. He'd already nearly ruined my life once, and I wanted nothing to do with him a second time. He honestly expected me to welcome him back into the family with open arms and help him get on with his life." She shook her head. "I couldn't do that."

"How did he almost ruin your life?" Ashley asked.

Sassie waved her hand at Ashley. "That's all water under the bridge. It has nothing to do with anything."

Ashley wrapped both hands around her bottle of water. "Mother, you can be so evasive."

"I'll give you the information you need, but I'm not going to dig up old hurts from years ago."

Ashley's eyes sparked with anger. "First of all, you've never given me what I needed as far as information, and second of all, you're the one who brought up old hurts by saying that Ernest nearly ruined your life."

"Well," Sassie said, "clearly, considering what's going on, I shouldn't have said that. I should have chosen my words more carefully."

There was an awkward silence, and Joy decided to change the topic. "How about your old friend in the hospital?"

"Yeah," Ashley said. "Cowboy Bob."

Shirley leaned forward. If she'd taken care of Bob, she couldn't—and wouldn't—say so. That would be confidential.

"You know, Mother." Ashley leaned back. "Your friend from Montana."

Sassie's face reddened. "What are you talking about?"

"You told me you were visiting an old friend in the hospital on Friday morning," Joy said. "And then I saw you go into a hospital room earlier today. A man came out of the room later, after you left. He wore a cowboy hat and said he was from Montana."

Sassie glanced out the window. "He's an old friend. From high school. I haven't seen him in over thirty years. He contacted me through the shop. He has cancer and came back to Charleston, on a sort of goodbye tour."

"What's his name?" Ashley asked.

"Robert Chorro. He goes by Bob." It *was* the same man.

Ashley's voice grew louder. "Do Hannah and Parker know him?"

Sassie didn't answer.

Ashley's face reddened, and the cords in her neck tightened.

"How about if everyone pauses for a minute and we all take a deep breath?" Shirley's voice was calm. She took a deep breath. As she took another one, Joy joined her. As she took a third, Ashley joined her too. After they all took a fourth, Sassie finally joined in too. After several more deep breaths, Shirley said, "All right. You can continue, Ashley. But if you start to feel out of control, pause and take a couple of deep breaths."

Ashley took another deep breath and then repeated her question. "Do Hannah and Parker know Cowboy Bob?"

"They didn't keep in touch either," Sassie answered.

Ashley continued. "Do Hannah and Parker know Ernest?"

"They did, way back when."

Joy couldn't help but wonder what had happened between Sassie and her cousin.

Ashley leaned farther back in her chair. "Does all of this have anything to do with my father?"

"Of course not," Sassie said.

"Because over thirty years ago sounds like around the time I was born."

"Yes, you were born over thirty years ago. Thirty-four years to be exact. But that has nothing to do with any of this. It's purely coincidental."

"How about Parker's claim that you poisoned Hannah?" Joy asked. "What's in the special formula that you use?"

Sassie brushed her hair behind her ear and then took a long drink of tea. Then she stood. "I've answered enough of your irrelevant questions. I'll see you tomorrow, Joy."

Shirley stood too.

Sassie held up her hand. "I appreciate your intervention. Your professionalism, Shirley. But I can't answer any more questions." Sassie didn't say anything to Ashley as she left the room and marched down the hall. The front door opened and closed firmly. Joy hadn't had a chance to ask her if Sassie was a nickname or her given name.

"I'm sorry," Joy said.

"So am I," Shirley added.

Ashley pushed back from the table. "She gets this way. Secretive. Evasive. She's been this way my entire life. I shouldn't have brought up my father. It puts her in a fight-or-flight mode—but she never fights. She only flees."

That sounded significant to Joy. Sassie seemed like such a strong person, and yet she hadn't fought Parker's accusations. She hadn't fought the questioning. Instead, she'd fled. Most likely she was going back to hide in the Crane House, once again.

Chapter Ten

SHIRLEY AND JOY WALKED BACK to the hospital parking garage, where both of their cars were parked. "What do you think of Sassie's response to Ashley's questions?" Joy asked.

"I'm wondering what happened to her to make her run away like that."

"She obviously has something to hide." Joy pressed the walk button.

"That very well could be," Shirley responded. "But I'm guessing she has some sort of trauma in her past. Her flight response definitely kicked in."

Joy thought for a moment. "I agree. It could be both. Who knows how what happened thirty-five years ago affected her? She was young, single, and pregnant. And then an unwed mother. Long before that, her father died in Vietnam."

"Interesting." Shirley stepped into the street once the signal changed, followed by Joy. "She likely had abandonment issues as a child. Then Ashley's father didn't stick around. Perhaps that triggered her past losses."

Joy furrowed her brow as she walked alongside Shirley. When they reached the hospital she said, "I appreciate your insight into Sassie."

"Try not to corner her," Shirley said. "It's one thing for Ashley to get frustrated with her, but you should do your best to be a calming force."

"The good cop?" Joy smiled.

Shirley grinned. "Exactly."

"I also appreciated your breathing exercise," Joy said. "I'm going to remember that."

"It's a technique I use to get through hard shifts. We all need to remember to stop and breathe at some point." Shirley gave Joy a wry smile. "Sometimes multiple times a day."

Joy had always admired nurses, but it wasn't until she started working at Mercy and became Shirley's friend that she truly began to understand the sacrifices they made, both physically and emotionally, to save and care for others. It was a hard and oftentimes undervalued job. Not only did Shirley have a tough role as a float nurse, she was also caring for her aging mother, Regina, who'd had her own illustrious career as a nurse at Mercy years ago.

"I'm parked on the second level," Shirley said as they reached the parking garage.

"I'm on the first." Joy gave Shirley a hug. "Thank you so much for your support. I don't know what I'd do without you."

"Aww." Shirley gave Joy a big squeeze. "I feel the same way."

"Tell your mother hello," Joy said as she let go of her friend.

"I will. She's praying for Sabrina. We both are. Let me know when she's discharged." Shirley grinned.

"Yes, ma'am." Joy returned the smile. "I definitely will."

As Joy walked to her car, her phone rang in her purse. She quickly dug it out, expecting a call from Sabrina. But it was Ashley.

"Hello," Joy said. "Everything all right?"

"Mostly," Ashley said. "Except Hannah's been trying to get ahold of Parker, but he's not answering his phone. She's being discharged. I can't get ahold of Mother either, even though she just left my place. And my car is in the shop."

"I can help," Joy said. "I'm in the parking garage."

Ten minutes later, Joy waited in her Mini Cooper outside the door where patients were discharged. She had the car in park and music on, playing softly. She expected to wait for a while, but immediately Lance wheeled Hannah out the door, with Ashley walking behind them, carrying a bouquet of flowers and a balloon.

Ashley pointed to Joy's car, and Lance wheeled Hannah to the passenger side. As he opened the door, Joy said, "Hello, Lance. Hello, Hannah."

Lance squinted and then smiled. "Hello, Miss Joy."

Joy waved.

Lance stepped back while Hannah climbed into the passenger seat. She wore capris and a summer top, the same clothes she wore on Friday. When Hannah didn't say thank you, Joy called out, "Thank you, Lance!"

He smiled and waved.

Ashley stuffed the balloon into the back seat and then climbed in with the bouquet of flowers—a gorgeous arrangement of sunflowers, yellow and orange roses, and lilies.

"Who are the flowers from?" Joy asked.

Hannah stared straight ahead. "Parker."

Joy pulled away from the hospital. "Ashley said you live on Sullivan's Island."

"Yes. Turn right at the third street after going over the bridge."

"Any word about your lab work?" Joy asked Hannah.

She shook her head. "Parker's working on it."

They drove in silence after that. When Joy glanced in the rearview mirror, Ashley was staring out her window, her face barely visible over the flowers, a wistful expression on her face.

Even though Sullivan's Island was northwest of the hospital, across the bay, Joy had to drive through downtown to the parkway and across the Ravenel Bridge, a cable bridge that spanned the Cooper River.

Joy loved the bridge. The four white pyramids created by the cables gave it a sense of whimsy and the sense of transporting from one world to another—or more accurately from Charleston to Mount Pleasant. She turned south and after a few minutes came to the Ben Sawyer Bridge, the passage to Sullivan's Island.

When they crossed, Joy counted three streets and turned. Then she asked, "Now what?"

"Keep going."

To the left was the Sullivan's Island Lighthouse. Just as they passed it, Hannah said, "Turn here."

Joy did.

"Take the next right."

Joy turned onto a narrow lane.

"It's ahead."

The house was a modern design with a walkout basement plus three stories. The structure seemed unusually wide, most likely providing a view of the ocean from nearly every room.

"You can park in front of the garage," Hannah said. "Right side."

It was a triple garage, dug out of the earth and tucked under the bottom of the house. An outside staircase led to a back deck and door.

Joy parked and shut off the engine. She climbed out of the car, walked around to the other side, and took the vase of flowers from Ashley.

From the deck above them, Lindsay called out, "Mom. What are you doing home so soon?"

Hannah looked up at Lindsay. "I was discharged."

"Where's Dad?"

"I don't know," Hannah said. "Did he have a business meeting this afternoon?"

"He left a couple of hours ago. I thought he was going to visit you." Lindsay shrugged. "I just made a cheese plate. There's enough for everyone."

"Oh, we should get going," Joy said, not wanting to intrude.

"Please come on up," Hannah said. "I could use the distraction."

Joy glanced at Ashley over the flowers. Ashley nodded, the balloon in her hand bouncing up and down with her head.

Hannah led the way. The yard was gorgeous, and Joy thought of the book Hannah had with her Friday on gardening. A paved pathway led to a fountain. Off to the side was a covered area with an island, fireplace, barbecue, and sectional. Beyond the living area was a swimming pool. When they reached the deck and then the door, Lindsay motioned them all inside through a back porch complete with counters, a sink, cupboards, and closets.

Lindsay went up a staircase that led straight to the kitchen, a great room, and an amazing view of the Atlantic that took Joy's breath away.

"Goodness," Joy said. "Have you gotten used to this view?"

Hannah said, "Almost," as Lindsay said, "Never."

"You've lived here nearly your whole life," Ashley said. "This is all you know."

Lindsay shook her head. "I know how to be grateful. I don't take it for granted. Nothing stays the same forever, right? I'll move away. Somebody might offer Dad ten million for this place, and we all know he'd sell it out from under us in a hot minute. I'll be grateful for it while I can."

Joy liked the girl even more.

Lindsay turned to Hannah. "Mom, do you feel all right? Do you need to rest?"

"I'm fine," Hannah said. "Cheese and crackers sound great."

"It's a cheeseboard, Mom." Lindsay put her hands on her hips. "Not just cheese and crackers."

On the kitchen counter was a platter with four different cheeses, olives, dried cherries, slices of baguette, and chocolate almonds.

"I may have gotten carried away." Lindsay laughed. "It's a good thing y'all showed up."

Lindsay pulled four plates from the cupboard and then grabbed a stack of napkins and started for the sectional in the sitting area that had a large, low table in front of it. A phone buzzed.

"That's me," Lindsay said. She pulled her cell from her back pocket, and a girl's face appeared.

"Linds," the girl said. "Can you explain that assignment to me now?"

"Sure. Hold on." Lindsay said to Ashley and Joy, "I'm a summer school tutor. This is going to take a while."

"No worries," Ashley said.

Lindsay filled a plate for herself and then headed for the staircase.

While they got their food, Joy asked Hannah, "Do you feel up to answering some questions?"

"Sure," Hannah said.

"Do you know anything about an old friend of Sassie's? A Robert Chorro? He goes by Bob."

Hannah shook her head. "No. I've never heard her mention anyone by that name."

"He's from Montana."

Hannah paused a moment and then said, "I've never heard Sassie mention anyone from Montana."

Ashley nodded. "That's what I thought too. But Bob Chorro, who's from Montana, claims to be an old friend of Mother's. And she's been visiting him in the hospital."

"How odd," Hannah said.

"How about Sassie's cousin, Ernest Crane?" Joy asked. "Have you heard anything from him recently?"

"Ernest?" Hannah held a cracker in midair. "Is he back home?"

"Perhaps," Joy answered.

Hannah shook her head. "We haven't seen him or heard from him in years."

"How many years?" Joy asked.

"At least twenty."

It sounded as if they'd seen him after he was released from prison the first time.

"What happened between Ernest and Sassie?" Joy asked. "Over thirty years ago?"

Hannah glanced at Ashley and then back at Joy. "You should ask Sassie."

"We have asked her," Ashley said. "She's doing that secretive, evasive thing that she does."

Hannah shrugged. "I don't remember a lot from back then, but it's really not my place to talk about it. You should ask Sassie again."

Joy, feeling awkward, said, "It seems that Ernest Crane may have been spotted Friday morning. I'd like to explore that more, considering Sassie seems to think whoever stole the safe is the same person who hit Sabrina."

"I understand that," Hannah said. "And perhaps this is a coincidence too, but Ernest used to have an auto body shop in the Crane Building warehouse. He could have easily known about that safe—in fact I'm pretty sure he used it to hide the money from the cars he stole."

"Interesting," Joy said.

"He served six years," Hannah said. "He didn't come back to Charleston for another five years after that. Then he was incarcerated for something else, although I have no idea what."

"I have another question," Joy said. "What is Sassie's given name?"

"Given name?" Hannah lifted her chin. "Sassie is her given name, isn't it? I've never heard her go by anything else. I've never seen another name."

"All right," Joy said.

Lindsay came down the stairs, holding two phones in her hand.

"Dad left his cell in the office," she said, handing it to her mother. "Why would he do that?"

Hannah held out her hand and took the phone. "I have no idea. You know how he's been lately. He probably just forgot it."

Lindsay didn't look convinced.

That evening, once she was home, Joy texted Sabrina to see how she was feeling.

THE SAME, she texted back. GOING TO SLEEP NOW. TALK TO YOU IN THE MORNING.

SWEET DREAMS. I LOVE YOU.

Sabrina "loved" Joy's text but didn't respond. Her headache wasn't any better. Was the pool of blood pressing against her brain growing larger? What would happen if she needed surgery and they didn't do it soon enough?

Joy couldn't shake her anxiety. She made herself a cup of mint tea and headed outside to her garden, settling on Wilson's bench under the magnolia tree. Tears stung her eyes, and her heart began to race.

Her love for Sabrina was as strong as the coastal tides. And as reliable. She was also well aware that her fear could be as destructive as a gale force wind.

After taking a deep breath and exhaling slowly, Joy said out loud, "God is in charge." His ways weren't her ways, and she needed to trust Him. She had a choice—she could trust Him or not. The alternative was fear—which wasn't good for her or Sabrina or Rob or Eloise or Mallory. Her fear could cause them all to falter. Even if she had to check herself every waking minute, she needed to trust the Lord.

She took a sip of tea as her thoughts drifted to the winter she lost Wilson. Joy knew better than anyone that life could change in a minute. Like Lindsay, she knew not to take anything for granted. It was true that nothing stayed the same. But all Joy asked was that Sabrina would outlive her. By thirty or more years, at least.

Trust. She had to. But trusting meant accepting life's ups and downs. That wasn't always an easy process. She'd had a bumpy time with that after Wilson died.

Trust.

Sabrina had to make it.

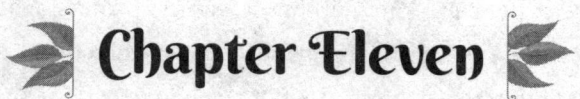

Chapter Eleven

THE NEXT MORNING, JOY TRIED the door of Sassie's salon at 6:25. It was locked. No lights were on inside.

Six thirty. 6:33. Joy imagined Sassie sitting in her sunroom, staring at the ceiling. Finally, at 6:34, Sassie swung the door open. "Why are you standing out here?"

"The door was locked."

"Oh." Sassie fiddled with the doorknob. "It's unlocked now. Come on in."

Joy followed Sassie through the lobby, which was dark, past the desk, and into the styling room. Sassie pointed to the first chair. Joy put her purse in the open cupboard and then climbed up in the chair.

Sassie draped the nylon cape around Joy's shoulders and fastened it in the back. "How do you like your color?"

"I like it," Joy answered. "I've gotten quite a few compliments on it."

"Wonderful." Sassie leaned Joy back to wash her hair. "That's what I love to hear. Now how about your cut?"

"I like the style I have—just clean it up."

"All right," Sassie said. "How about if I add some texture to your bangs?"

"Sounds good."

"And make it just a tad shorter, for summer?"

"Okay," Joy said. "But not much shorter."

Sassie was talkative and chipper. Nothing like she'd been the day before in her sunroom. Perhaps it was her professional persona, but she seemed even more gregarious than she had on Friday.

Joy hated to break the mood, but she had questions that needed answers. Sassie finished rinsing Joy's hair and wrapped a towel around it. Joy sat up. "Ashley said there's no henna in the shop, that she's never seen any, but both Hannah and Parker claim that the special formula for Hannah's hair dye contains henna."

Joy watched Sassie's expression in the mirror.

She didn't flinch. "Hannah wanted something special, something as natural as possible. I'd experimented with henna on her hair when we were younger, but the color I eventually came up with is entirely manufactured. It was so rich and perfect for her, Hannah assumed I added henna to it—but you actually can't mix henna and hair dye. It doesn't work." Sassie wrapped a towel around Joy's neck. "But Hannah told everyone I came up with an original color for her and when I said I didn't, Hannah thought I was being modest. Or maybe the thought of her own 'Sassie trademark' formula made her feel special, and she didn't want to give that up and accept that there was nothing original about it." Sassie began combing out Joy's hair. "After a while I stopped trying to correct her."

"Who knew about the formula theory?"

"Everyone," Sassie said. "Honestly, Hannah—along with Parker—were my biggest marketers, strictly by word of mouth."

"Was there anything different about the dye you used on Friday?"

"Nothing." Sassie opened a drawer and took out a pair of scissors. "And it's ludicrous for anyone to think that I poisoned her. There's nothing I could put in hair dye that would poison her that quickly."

"But how about over time?"

"Well, sure, that's a possibility." Sassie looked over her shoulder as she talked to Joy. "I've actually read about that—not a hairdresser purposefully poisoning someone but accidently poisoning them by putting in too much phenylenediamine. But premade formulas—which I use—wouldn't have levels high enough to do any damage."

"That makes sense," Joy said. It didn't mean Sassie couldn't have added more phenylenediamine to the dye. It also didn't mean she did.

Joy shivered. A hairdresser could commit murder in all sorts of ways. Too much phenylenediamine. Or too much ammonia.

"Would you like some coffee?" Sassie asked. "It smells like the pot is done."

"No, thank you," Joy said. "I already had one cup—and I'll get another when I get to work."

Or a hairdresser could put something in a drink.

Joy thought again of Hannah's water bottle—but Sassie hadn't given Hannah anything to drink. And the smell of ammonia hadn't been in the air. Joy would have noticed that, plus it would have affected her and everyone else in the shop too.

Joy remained silent for a few moments. Sassie moved deftly as she cut Joy's hair.

"I'm curious about your name," Joy said. "Is Sassie a nickname?"

Sassie shook her head. "It's my legal name."

Joy smiled at her in the mirror. "So you've been Sassie since birth?"

Sassie laughed. "Very sassy."

Joy laughed too. "But did you change your name to S-a-s-s-i-e legally?"

Sassie's scissors stilled. "Yes, I changed it to my legal name."

"What was your birth name?"

Sassie smiled. "My, you're awfully nosy—especially for so early in the morning."

"You're right," Joy said. "I *am* being nosy." She chuckled. "Perhaps my manners haven't woken up yet."

Sassie met Joy's eyes in the mirror and said, "You're forgiven."

Internally, Joy admitted defeat as far as the name issue—at least for now.

Joy changed the subject, asking how many clients Sassie had booked for the day.

"It's a full day," Sassie said. "At least ten. But I need to check the schedule to know for sure. Ashley worked in a few of my cancellations from Saturday."

Joy hesitated, wondering if she'd pushed Sassie too far with the nickname questions. She pressed on. "Evelyn remembers a young man named Riley from thirty years ago that she thinks was a part of your circle."

"Oh?" Sassie continued snipping Joy's hair. "What did Evelyn say about him?"

"That he ended up in the hospital." Joy stopped, not wanting to say too much.

Sassie continued cutting. "All of that was so long ago. I don't remember much...." Her voice trailed away.

If Joy pushed the topic, she guessed Sassie would say it was coincidental that Riley had been poisoned and now Parker was claiming that Hannah had been. But then again, Hannah might not have been poisoned at all. And a poisoning over thirty years ago would hold little significance today.

A half hour later as Joy walked through the gift shop, she stopped at the mirror next to the hats and evaluated her haircut. It was a little shorter and a little more textured, along with—of course—a little lighter than usual. She smiled. She'd told Sassie she liked it—and she did, even more so on second inspection.

She continued on to the back room. She had an hour to ready the shop for opening—but first she'd text Sabrina. GOOD MORNING. HOW ARE YOU FEELING?

THE SAME, Sabrina texted back. I HAVE A CT SCAN THIS MORNING.

DO YOU WANT ME TO COME UP?

NO. I'M DOING OKAY. I KNOW YOU NEED TO OPEN THE SHOP.

Joy fought her sense of panic. Sabrina wasn't feeling any better. What would the next CT show? She inhaled deeply, exhaled slowly, and then concentrated on her list of tasks.

At eight o'clock on the dot, as Joy flipped the sign to open, her phone buzzed in her pocket. It was a Houston number but not one in her contacts. Thinking it was a friend who'd gotten a new phone number, Joy answered.

But just in case it was a business call, she said, "Joy Atkins speaking."

"This is Stanley Marks, an attorney in Houston. I work for Daybreak Oil and Gas."

That was the company Wilson had worked for. At the time of his death, he'd been there for thirty-five years. Why would an attorney from Wilson's old company be calling her? Joy frowned. "How may I help you?"

"You can't," Mr. Marks said. "I'm helping you. I wanted to notify you that Daybreak Oil and Gas is suing the estate of Wilson S. Atkins…" It was obvious he was reading a statement. "…for embezzlement. You'll receive a letter explaining our investigation and asking for documents from your accountant to compare with ours."

"Wh-what?" Joy stammered.

"Read the letter when it arrives. It will explain—"

"Please email me a copy of the letter now," Joy said.

"That's not possible."

"Mr. Marks, of course it's possible. Email it now." She rattled off her email address.

"I'll ask my assistant to put it on her to-do list for today."

"Tell her to do it now," Joy said. "I will not let another minute go by with the integrity of my late husband in question."

"Good day, Mrs. Atkins."

"Now!" Joy commanded as he hung up.

Joy immediately dialed the direct line of their family lawyer, Carlos Martin, at his practice in Houston, and left a voice mail. Then she checked her email. There was nothing from the oil company.

Carlos had been a young lawyer who'd just passed the Texas State Bar when Wilson hired him to draw up a will right before Sabrina was born. Carlos did general law but specialized in estate planning. He handled Wilson's parents' estate and then Joy's parents' estate as well.

Over the years Wilson and Joy brought Carlos their own business, along with the business of their friends, neighbors, and several colleagues from Wilson's work as well, which Carlos had been grateful for. Over time he became a family friend as well as a trusted lawyer. He'd been invaluable to Joy after Wilson died.

Next, Joy called their family accountant, who was also in Houston. She'd advised Joy about where to invest Wilson's life insurance and retirement accounts after he passed away. The profit from their Houston home, along with a portion of Wilson's insurance money, had gotten Joy into the house in Charleston. His remaining insurance money, retirement money, and investments assured her a comfortable retirement and set aside emergency funds for herself and Sabrina.

She expected the call to go to the accountant's voice mail since it was so early, but she answered. "Randi McMillan, how may I help you?"

Joy quickly explained the phone call from the oil company attorney. "I'll get together all of the records I have," Joy said.

"Wait until you talk to your attorney," Randi advised. "They'll need a subpoena for any financial records."

"I know Wilson didn't embezzle money. The sooner I can prove that the better."

"But there's a correct way to go about it," Randi said. "You have no idea what that is."

That was true. "You're right," Joy said. "I'll wait until I speak with my attorney."

"Good," Randi said. "These things happen."

"What do you mean 'these things happen'? That people are falsely accused of embezzling, after they've passed away?"

Randi hesitated and then said, "Well, I haven't had that exact scenario happen with a client. But I have had some accused of embezzlement."

"And they were all innocent?"

"No," Randi said. "They weren't all innocent."

Joy inhaled sharply. "Well, Wilson is innocent. There's no way he stole—not from anybody but especially not from his company."

"Yes," Randi said. "I'm sure you're right. I can't imagine Wilson as an embezzler either. Let me know what I can do after you learn more."

Joy thanked Randi and ended the call.

Could she be wrong about Wilson?

No. Still, just the accusation made her hand shake as she ended the call.

The sound of someone clearing their throat startled her.

"What was that all about?" Ashley asked.

Joy responded by asking her, "What are you doing here so early?"

"I was out on my morning walk and thought I'd stop and check with you to see how Sabrina is doing."

Joy exhaled. "She's feeling the same—she'll have another scan this morning."

Ashley pointed to Joy's cell phone, which she still held in her hand. "Sorry to eavesdrop, but that call sounded pretty intense. What's going on?"

"I'm not sure yet," Joy said.

"A family mystery?"

"Perhaps," Joy answered.

Ashley smiled. "Welcome to the club."

Joy grimaced but then regrouped. "I'm still thinking about your mother's name. Is there a family name that might have been her given name?"

Ashley gave her questioning look.

"Your middle name? Your great-grandmother Crane's name? That sort of thing."

"I have no idea what my great-grandmother's name was. No one ever talked about her. But my middle name is Marie."

Joy pursed her lips. "And so is your mother's, right?"

Ashley laughed. "That isn't helpful, is it? Marie Marie would be her name if that theory worked."

Joy agreed with Ashley's assessment without joining her in laughter.

Between customers, Joy dusted the glassware. More people bought Father's Day cards—and each time she said a blessing over them. She often checked her phone to see if she'd missed a text or call from Sabrina or Rob or an email from the attorney. When her phone finally dinged, she checked it immediately. It was a text from Hope, asking how Sabrina was doing.

THE SAME, Joy texted back.

Joy continued checking her phone for the next half hour and, finally, the email came through. She immediately forwarded it to her accountant and her lawyer with instructions to listen to the voice mail she left and to call her back ASAP.

When the next customer came in, Joy forced herself to smile. All she wanted to do was attend to her family—to the accusations against Wilson, and to Sabrina. The man chose a Get Well card and a Father's Day card, paid, and then left. Joy said a blessing for him and his family as well, both for Father's Day and for healing. Why hadn't she been praying for healing all along when people purchased Get Well cards? She'd start doing that too.

Evelyn stopped in for a cup of coffee at nine. Joy was tempted to tell her about the accusation against Wilson but decided to wait until she had more information. After Evelyn checked on how Sabrina was doing, as she poured her coffee, she asked, "Any new clues as far as the possible poisoning, theft, and hit-and-run?"

"Nothing useful," Joy answered. "Sassie evaded my questions about Riley, saying it was a long time ago."

"Really?" Evelyn wrapped both hands around her mug. "I got the impression back then that she and Riley were rather close but that her grandfather didn't approve of him. The grandfather also didn't approve of Sassie opening a beauty salon—he thought it was beneath her—but he really didn't approve of her friendship with Riley." Evelyn took a sip of coffee.

"Why not?"

"He was from North Carolina. Up in the hills. He moved to Charleston to stay with a relative. He was poor as a church mouse. No family to speak of. No future."

"Interesting." Joy poured herself a cup of coffee. "Especially considering that Cousin Ernest ended up in prison."

"Right?" Evelyn took another sip of coffee. "All families have their problems."

Joy winced as she thought of the accusations against Wilson.

Evelyn asked, "Any luck finding out if Sassie is a nickname?"

"Sassie said she made it her legal name. But she wouldn't tell me when she changed it or what her birth name was. But I have some ideas to investigate. I'm wondering what some of the family names are. Ashley told me Marie is both her and Sassie's middle name, so obviously it's not Sassie's real first name. We should look into Sassie's mother's name and her grandmother's—especially her grandmother on the Crane side."

"Good idea," Evelyn said. "I can research marriage licenses for Sassie's grandparents and her parents on my break."

"Thank you," Joy said. "That would be great."

Evelyn left with her cup of coffee, and Joy continued on with her work. Just before nine thirty her phone rang. It was her attorney. Thankfully no customers were in the shop, and she stepped back by the coffee maker to take the call.

Carlos explained that he'd gotten her voice mail and the email. "I've read the letter," he said. "If you don't turn over your financial documents, they'll most likely get a subpoena."

"Do they have reason for suspicion?" Joy asked.

"I'd say their reasons are valid. Wilson was the treasurer of the company and had access to the money. A large chunk is missing from his department, and the entry dates on the transfers indicate he was still alive at that time."

"Do the entries show where the money went?"

"No. That information was hidden." Carlos paused for a moment and then said, "You need to show that he didn't take it."

"All right," Joy said.

"I'll contact the attorney who wrote the letter and then contact your accountant—I still have her information. I'll let you know what I come up with."

"Thank you," Joy said. She told Carlos about Sabrina's accident. "I'm a little preoccupied right now, but we really need to prove Wilson's innocence."

"Of course," Carlos answered. "If you can't pick up my calls, I'll leave detailed messages."

Joy thanked him again and ended the call, grateful Carlos could begin working on this immediately but still unsettled about the entire situation.

Just before ten her phone dinged again. This time it was Rob. SURGERY NEEDED AND WILL BE DONE IMMEDIATELY. CAN YOU COME UP TO SABRINA'S ROOM ASAP?

Chapter Twelve

Joy hit the four button in the elevator once and then again. And then a third time.

"Are you all right?"

She turned. A man with a bald head and the beginnings of a goatee stood in the corner of the elevator. He wore jeans and a plain navy T-shirt.

"Just a little anxious," she replied. The man seemed familiar, but she couldn't place him. She stared down at the floor. She'd just found out that her deceased husband was suspected of embezzlement, and now that her only child was going to have to have brain surgery.

Joy raised her gaze to the ascending numbers on the elevator. She stepped out at her floor and squared her shoulders. She would be nothing but strong for Sabrina—she wouldn't show a hint of fear. All would be well. She truly believed that.

She hurried down the hall.

Rob stood on one side of the bed, and Reverend Neal stood on the other. Reverend Neal stepped back, making room for Joy.

"Mom," Sabrina said. "You're here. Who's watching the shop?"

"Anne," Joy answered. "She said she can stay until Lacy arrives at noon." Lacy was Joy's main volunteer, and she worked a couple of times a week. "She'll pick up Eloise and Mallory as planned but won't tell them about the surgery—if Rob hasn't already." Joy stepped to Sabrina's side. "How are you?"

"Relieved. I want to get this over with. All these scans and headaches and waiting are wearing me down."

Joy nodded. That was understandable. "How are the girls doing?"

Rob said, "We haven't told them yet. We figured we'd tell them after the surgery is over, once they're done with camp for the day."

That was understandable too.

There was a knock on the door, and someone called out, "Transportation."

"Come in," Rob called.

Lance stepped into the room. He smiled at Sabrina. "Ready?"

"Yes," Sabrina said.

Reverend Neal asked, "Do we have time for a prayer?"

"Of course." Lance bowed his head. "We always have time for prayer."

Reverend Neal prayed for Sabrina, for the surgeon, and for healing. Then he prayed for Rob, the girls, and for Joy. "Lord, we pray that, above all else, all of us would trust You today. Amen."

"Amen," Joy echoed.

She bent down and gave Sabrina a hug and then kissed her forehead. "I love you, baby."

"I love you too, Mom."

Joy stepped aside as Rob hugged and spoke with Sabrina.

"How are you holding up?" Lance asked Joy.

"All right." She gave him a smile, but she felt as weak as a newborn.

He patted her on the shoulder and said, "I'll be praying for Sabrina the rest of the day."

"Thank you," Joy answered.

As Joy moved toward the door, Sabrina said, "I don't want them to shave my head. Will I have time to talk to the surgeon about that?"

Lance smiled, his eyes bright. "You can try."

Joy stepped out of the room and out of the way to wait. The man she'd seen earlier in the elevator, who had asked if she was all right, exited Cowboy Bob's room. He walked with his chin down and either didn't see her or chose not to acknowledge her. He approached the elevator.

Lance pushed Sabrina out of the room, followed by Rob and Reverend Neal. Lance was aiming for the staff elevator as Amanda stepped out. She waved at Joy and Rob and then went back in the elevator with Sabrina while the others ambled toward the visitor elevator. The man who came out of Cowboy Bob's room was already gone.

Amanda met Rob and Joy in the surgery waiting room. "How are the two of you doing?" she asked.

"All right," Joy answered, with Rob echoing.

Amanda gave each of them a hug. "Sabrina is in good hands. Dr. Reynolds is very, very good at what he does. And Sabrina is calm and collected. I don't have any worries."

That warmed Joy. It was such a relief to have Dr. Amanda Taylor around during medical crises. She'd been a big help after Wilson collapsed and during the two days before he died.

"Call me if you need anything," Amanda said. "I'll be finishing rounds and then I have appointments this afternoon, but I can get right back to you."

A half hour later, Dr. Reynolds stepped into the waiting room to speak with Rob and Joy. "Sabrina is being wheeled into surgery right now," he said. "I'm on my way to scrub." He smiled. "She instructed me that she doesn't want her head shaved, and I assured her we'll do our best." He turned to Rob. "We talked about the surgery a couple of days ago. Do you have any questions?"

Rob shook his head. "You explained it well before."

Dr. Reynolds put his hand on Rob's shoulder. "It should take a couple of hours. If it takes longer, one of the nurses will let you know. I'll come out and speak to you as soon as the surgery is done."

"Thank you," Joy said.

And then they waited. Rob texted Anne and thanked her for picking up the girls from the camp.

"I'll get them from Anne's later," Joy said.

"That sounds like a good plan," Rob said. He scrolled through his phone while Joy texted Hope, Evelyn, Shirley, and Ashley, requesting that all of them pray. Each one texted back immediately. Shirley had the day off and asked if Joy wanted her to come sit with her. Joy responded that at the moment, no thank you, but that she'd let her know if that changed. Ashley asked if they needed help with the girls. Joy texted back, No, BUT THANK YOU. Evelyn said she'd stop by the waiting room in a few minutes. Joy texted back, THANK YOU.

Shortly, Evelyn arrived with coffees for both Rob and Joy. She said she was praying for Sabrina and each of them and then left. A half hour later, Ashley carried in sandwiches from the deli a block away. She made sure they had everything they needed and then slipped out. An hour later, Shirley and her mother, Regina, arrived with an assortment of cookies from Oceanside Bakery, which was in the neighborhood.

"We're praying for Sabrina," Regina said as she hugged Joy. Next, she hugged Rob. "You hang in there. Don't stop trusting God."

"I won't," Rob said. Regina sat down on the other side of Rob and took his hand.

Shirley sat down next to Joy. "Are you okay?"

"I'm all right," Joy said. "I'm thankful for a skilled surgeon." Her words caught in her throat and threatened to break apart into a sob. She didn't want to do that to Rob.

After Shirley and Regina left, Joy checked her phone. It was past noon. Lacy should be at the shop now, and Anne would be on her way to pick up the girls.

She put her phone in her lap as the man she'd seen earlier on the elevator passed through the waiting room. She stared at his bald head and the stubble on his chin. Was he the guy who followed Sassie through the lobby Friday morning? Could he be the hair product rep that stopped in the salon on Friday afternoon? He might have shaved his head and goatee—and was now growing the latter back.

Joy stared at him as he exited the waiting room and reviewed what she knew. He had come out of Cowboy Bob's room. Evelyn thought she'd seen Sassie's cousin Ernest. Sassie had a reaction to seeing the man in the lobby. The hair product rep was an imposter.

She googled *Charles Ernest Crane* again and looked at the mug shot from ten years before. The guy had gray hair and a goatee. His face was fuller, but perhaps he'd lost weight. Joy texted the photo to Evelyn. IS THIS THE MAN YOU SAW IN THE LOBBY FRIDAY MORNING?

Perhaps, Evelyn texted back. Any word on Sabrina?

Not yet.

An hour later, Rob received a text from a nurse assisting Dr. Reynolds that the surgery was taking a little longer than anticipated. He showed the text to Joy. A second text appeared. As soon as we're done, Dr. Reynolds will come and speak with you.

Anxiety gripped Joy's chest. She exhaled slowly and then said, "None of this means anything is wrong."

"I know," he said. Then he put his arm around her. "I sure am glad you're here."

"I wouldn't be anywhere else," Joy replied.

Ten minutes later, Eloise texted Rob from Anne's phone. How is Mommy? What's going on?

He showed it to Joy. "What should I tell her?"

"The truth," Joy said. "Call her and tell her her mommy is having surgery, that everything is going as planned, and you'll call as soon as you hear from the surgeon."

"What do I do if things don't go as planned?" Rob whispered.

"Things will go as planned. If they don't, we'll go to Anne's house, get the girls, and tell them whatever is going on."

He nodded. "You're right." He called Eloise and told her exactly what Joy had said.

Forty-five minutes later, Dr. Reynolds came through the door to surgery, still in scrubs, wearing booties over his shoes, and with his face mask hanging around his neck. "Sorry it took longer than expected. The surgery was a little more complicated than I anticipated, but everything went well."

Relief flooded through Joy.

"Sabrina is in recovery," Dr. Reynolds said. "You'll be able to see her within the hour."

"Thank you," Joy said.

"How long will she need to stay in the hospital?" Rob asked.

"I'm not sure. At least for tonight. I'll check on her this evening and then again in the morning."

Rob texted Anne's phone so the girls would have the good news while Joy texted Hope, Evelyn, Shirley, Ashley, and Amanda.

After she finished, she said to Rob, "Do you want to get something to eat before we go over to recovery?"

"I could use something cold to drink," he said.

"How about if you go to the cafeteria, and I'll stop by the shop and close it up. Then I'll meet you in recovery. After I see Sabrina, I'll go pick up the girls."

As Joy headed through the lobby on her way to the gift shop, Sassie came through the front door of the hospital. Joy called out, "Hello."

Sassie looked up and said, "I thought you'd be with Sabrina."

"I need to check in at the gift shop."

Sassie took a step nearer. "Ashley said Sabrina came through surgery well. What a relief."

"Yes, it is." Joy suddenly felt exhausted.

"I'm guessing they had to shave her head, at least partially. Tell her I'll try to smooth things over. It will be my contribution to her getting better."

"Thank you," Joy said. "That's very kind. Where are you headed?"

"Up to see Bob again. Hopefully he'll be discharged tomorrow."

"Will he head back to Montana?"

"Yes," Sassie said. "Although he may need to stay for a few more days to regain his strength."

"Will he stay with you?"

Sassie shook her head. "I don't think so."

"I hope he'll be feeling strong soon."

"So do I." Sassie studied her and then said, "Your hair really is cute."

Joy couldn't help but smile. "Thank you."

Lacy was finishing with a customer as Joy entered the shop. After the customer left, Lacy asked, "How are you holding up?"

"Great. Sabrina is doing well."

Lacy stepped out from behind the counter and gave Joy a hug.

"You can go ahead and go," Joy said. "It's only a half hour until closing. I'll do it and then go see Sabrina in recovery."

"Are you sure?" Lacy asked. "I can stick around."

"It'll at least be a half hour until I can see her. Then I'll go get the girls."

After Lacy left, Joy had three more customers. One, a woman about Joy's age, bought two Father's Day cards—one for her husband and one for her father. "My dad is ninety-seven," the woman said. After she left, Joy said a blessing for her family, fighting the urge to be jealous that the woman not only still had her husband but her father too.

As soon as it was three o'clock, Joy flipped the sign and headed for the back room. As she collapsed into a chair, she burst into tears of relief, realizing how fearful she'd been of losing Sabrina too. Yes, she trusted God. But the fear had still been there.

When Wilson collapsed, it seemed to take forever for the ambulance to arrive, but it had only been seven minutes. In no time they had him in the ambulance and she was in her car and on the way to the closest hospital, about ten minutes away. When she reached the emergency room, a doctor was already examining Wilson.

Joy let out another sob and then dried her eyes. She needed to go see Sabrina. And then call Carlos to see if he had any news for her. And then put on a brave face, go get her granddaughters, and live in the moment and focus on them.

She'd have time, later tonight, to cry again.

Amazingly, the right side of Sabrina's head wasn't completely shaved. The surgical team had been able to shave the under layer, leaving the long hair above. Sabrina would be pleased.

There was a dressing over the shaved part, and the long hair was pinned up on her head. The surgeon had been able to grant Sabrina's one wish.

Sabrina couldn't stay awake, and when she finally could, she cried out in pain. The nurse administered more pain meds, and then Sabrina fell back to sleep. Rob left momentarily to call Anne and check on the girls.

While he was gone, Sabrina woke back up. "Did they shave all of my hair?"

"No," Joy answered. "Just the under layer."

Sabrina smiled, just a little. She reached for Joy's hand and said, "I've been thinking about Daddy."

Tears stung Joy's eyes. "So have I."

"I'm sorry to put you through this again."

Joy squeezed Sabrina's hand. "*You* aren't putting me through anything. I'm sorry you were hit by that SUV. Mostly, I'm absolutely thankful you're going to be okay."

Sabrina closed her eyes. "It was so hard for me to lose Daddy as an adult. I didn't want my girls to have to live with the loss of a parent as children."

Joy nodded in agreement, even though Sabrina couldn't see her. "Yes," she murmured. "But there's no danger of them losing you. Everything is fine. You're going to be okay." Joy patted Sabrina's shoulder. "When Rob comes in, I'll go get the girls and take them home and feed them."

"Come see me in the morning, before you go to work."

"I will," Joy said. She wouldn't tell her about the phone call from the attorney from Daybreak Oil and Gas, or the letter, or the conversations with Carlos and Randi. All of that would have to wait.

A few minutes later, Rob returned, and Joy told him and Sabrina goodbye. Sabrina didn't open her eyes, but she waved and said, "Give the girls hugs and kisses from me. Tell them I'm doing fine."

Joy headed back to her house to get her car, dialing her lawyer on the way. Carlos didn't pick up, and she left a message. A couple of minutes later, as she climbed the steps to her house, he called her back. After saying hello, Carlos said, "I talked with the attorney at Daybreak and with your accountant, who has all of your tax records and investment statements. She has Wilson's retirement account statements at the time of his death but not his deposits through the years. Do you think you have those?"

"Probably," Joy answered, unlocking her front door.

"Check," he said. "And then let me know first thing in the morning. Leave a message tonight if you can. If you have them, I'll need copies ASAP."

"All right," Joy said. "I'll look this evening."

"Good. I'll talk with you tomorrow."

After Joy hung up, she poured herself a glass of water from the pitcher in the refrigerator and then squared her shoulders, ready to step out her door and into her car. And into her Mimi persona. It was time to go get her granddaughters and let them know their mother was going to be okay. But first she'd pick up a pizza and salad. She had no idea what there was to eat in the house.

By the time Joy and the girls arrived at Rob and Sabrina's house, it was nearly six o'clock. A neighbor had let Mopsy out at noon, but the poor dog was desperate to go out again. Joy opened the back door and Mopsy raced through, followed by Mallory.

Her phone rang. Shirley. Joy hit accept.

"How's Sabrina doing?" Shirley asked. "How are you?"

"Good and good," Joy answered. "I'm with the girls, at their house."

"Do you need dinner?"

"I picked up a pizza."

"Okay. I'm bringing dessert by. In half an hour."

"You don't need to do that," Joy said.

Shirley laughed. "Of course I do. Mama says so."

After Joy ended the call, Eloise asked, "Are you sure Mommy is okay?"

Joy nodded. "Like I said, I talked to her in the recovery room. She said to give you and Mallory hugs." Joy wrapped her arms around Eloise again. "And kisses." Joy kissed Eloise on the top of her head. "She wanted me to assure you she's all right."

"Can I talk to her?" Eloise asked.

Joy held out her phone. "Text your daddy and see what he says."

Eloise took the phone, and Joy went out the back door to bring Mopsy and Mallory in to eat their dinners. Rob texted Eloise right back, saying Sabrina was resting. He'd let Eloise know when she woke up.

A half hour later, a knock fell on the front door. Mallory ran to open it. Shirley stood on the porch, a pie carrier tucked under her arm, a bag in one hand, and purple and pink balloons in the other. "Ta-da!" she called out. "I come bearing gifts! And dessert!"

Mallory clapped her hands as they all made their way to the kitchen.

Shirley brought each of the girls a bouquet of balloons, Joy a bag of chocolates, and a strawberry pie with freshly whipped cream for all of them.

"Will you eat dessert with us?" Joy asked.

"Absolutely!" Shirley put the pie carrier on the kitchen counter and pulled the container of whipped cream from the bag.

Having Shirley stay for dessert distracted the girls. They chatted about sports camp—Monday was soccer and both of their teams had won. Mallory played goalie, and Eloise played midfield. Tomorrow was softball.

"Oh, I love softball," Shirley said. "I played catcher when I was your age."

"That's what I want to play!" Mallory spoke with her mouth full.

"Mallory," Joy said. "Swallow and then speak."

The conversation moved on to favorite desserts.

"Cotton candy!" Mallory shouted.

Eloise corrected her. "That's not a dessert."

"Cotton candy ice cream!"

Shirley laughed and then said, "How about you, Eloise? What's your favorite?"

"Mimi's peach cobbler."

"Goodness," Joy said. "I'm surprised you remember it."

"I don't remember it." Mallory crossed her arms.

"I'll make it sometime soon," Joy said. "Then you will."

"Yum," Shirley said. "Peach cobbler is a favorite of mine too."

Joy was tempted to tell Shirley about the accusation from Wilson's company. But she couldn't chance letting Eloise overhear, even if she could manage to find a few minutes with Shirley alone. Besides, they were all having so much fun. She didn't want to ruin it. But the burden of the accusation, heaped on top of Sabrina's surgery, felt excruciatingly heavy. Joy needed to tell someone soon.

Shirley helped Joy clean up. Then she said goodbye, leaving all three of them smiling from the cheery visit.

After the girls bathed, Rob texted to say Sabrina felt up to talking to them on the phone for a minute. NO VIDEO THOUGH, he texted. SABRINA CAN'T DO SCREENS AT ALL RIGHT NOW.

A minute later, Joy's phone rang. It was Rob. Joy put it on speaker and said, "Hello, you two. We're here."

"Hello," Sabrina said.

At the sound of her voice, Mopsy began to bark.

"Mommy," Eloise said. "How are you?"

The dog barked louder.

"Hi, Eloise. I'm fine. Mallory, are you there?"

The dog barked even louder.

"I'm going to take the dog out," Joy said.

"Mallory…"

Joy grabbed Mopsy's collar and dragged her to the back door. The dog kept turning her head toward the phone. "I'm sorry," Joy said, feeling horrible. But she wanted the girls to be able to talk with their mother.

A minute later, when she returned, Sabrina said, "Mallory" again.

"Answer Mommy," Eloise commanded.

"Hi, Mommy," Mallory whispered.

"How are you, baby?" Sabrina asked.

"All right… But I'm feeling shy."

"Mallory, it's me. Nothing has changed. There's no reason to be shy."

Joy sat down on the sectional and pulled Mallory onto her lap. Then she pulled Eloise close. "Mallory and Eloise," Joy said, "can you tell Mommy and Daddy about sports camp today? And your time with Anne and Addie."

As the girls began to warm up, telling Sabrina and Rob about playing a soccer tournament, Joy fought back tears once again. Sabrina was okay. The girls were resilient. Her attorney and lawyer would clear Wilson's good name.

Now, somehow, Joy would find out who hit Sabrina.

Chapter Thirteen

That night, after midnight, Joy wasn't as positive as she'd been earlier as she dug through cardboard boxes of files that she'd pulled from the spare bedroom closet to the middle of the room. She'd retrieved the files from Wilson's office at Daybreak after he passed away and then moved the files to Charleston, not thinking she would ever need them.

Finally, she came across a folder with the label Retirement Account, 1984. Behind it was Retirement Account, 1985. The last file was 2019. Bless Wilson for being so conscientious.

She hadn't looked at the files since right before she moved, and then it was just to transfer them into a cardboard box labeled 1984–2019. That was a lot of retirement, which was why Wilson's accounts were so robust. She double-checked the years. 1984 through 2011. Then 2013. Then 2015 through 2019. What had happened to 2012 and 2014? Joy searched through the box. Nothing.

Frustrated, she sat on the floor and leaned against the bed. Tears filled her eyes. Surely Daybreak Oil and Gas had records of all of Wilson's retirement investments that they paid into. Why was she digging for information they already had? But there were also his investments.

She opened the 1984 folder. There was only one blurry page. She blinked back her tears. She opened the 2019 file. There were three pages. For her to electronically scan all of the information would take quite a while. She sighed. But if it would help clear Wilson, it would be worth the time no matter how little sleep she managed to get.

She collected the files and headed into her office to do the scanning.

An hour later she'd finished and emailed the documents to Carlos, noting the absence of materials from 2012 and 2014 and assuring him she'd keep looking.

Once she was in bed, Joy stared at the ceiling, wide awake. She thought about Sabrina, how helpless she looked in recovery. How shaky her voice sounded over the phone as she talked with the girls.

Then she thought of Sassie. Did she know who stole the safe and hit Sabrina? What was she hiding? Then Joy's thoughts landed on Wilson and the accusation of the stolen retirement money.

The world felt heavy with injustice. That was why she felt so frustrated with Sassie. If she was hiding something that could lead to the driver who hit Sabrina—well, that felt like one more injustice.

Finally, she let the tears come. As they streamed down her temples and onto her pillow, she rolled to her side and reached for a tissue. As she continued to cry, holding the tissue to her face as she did, she fought back her fear. Sabrina had come through the surgery. She'd sort out the accusations against Wilson.

Still, she cried.

She breathed a prayer for comfort, for what she couldn't control, dried her tears one last time, and eventually drifted off to sleep.

The next morning Joy woke up a little late—at five forty-five instead of five thirty—feeling exhausted. After a cup of coffee, a shower, and a second cup of coffee, she felt halfway alive. She dressed in a blouse and capris, made a sandwich for her lunch, and hurried to the hospital to see Sabrina before it was time to open the gift shop.

As she walked to the hospital, she called Carlos and left a message that she'd scanned and emailed Wilson's investment information. "Check your email," she said.

Sabrina had been moved back to the fourth floor, to the same room she'd been in before. Rob had let Joy know that when he arrived home last night.

Visiting hours hadn't started yet, but Joy slipped through the lobby and to the empty elevator. When she reached Sabrina's room, she tiptoed inside to find her daughter sleeping. Joy stood at the end of the bed for a few minutes. It wasn't long until the nurse came in.

"How's she doing?" Joy whispered.

"She's on antibiotics," the nurse said. "She's been running a fever."

"That doesn't sound good."

The nurse shrugged. "It happens." She checked something on the monitor and then headed for the door. "Shift change. My replacement will be in soon."

Sabrina stirred a little but didn't wake. The surgery site was covered with gauze and she had an ice pack, wrapped in a cloth, on her pillow. Her face was pale.

It seemed at first that Wilson would be all right too after he collapsed on the kitchen floor. Joy fought the panic rising in her chest as she stared at Sabrina. And then she texted Amanda. ARE YOU AT THE HOSPITAL? SABRINA IS ON ANTIBIOTICS. I'M WORRIED. Joy hit send and then continued staring at her daughter.

A few minutes later, Amanda slipped into the room and put her arm around Joy. "It's not unusual to run a fever after surgery," she whispered. "They won't let her go home until they know everything is all right."

They hadn't let Wilson go home either—and he hadn't been all right.

Sabrina stirred again but this time she opened her eyes. She smiled. "What are you two doing?"

"Staring at you," Amanda answered.

"Do I have food in my teeth? A bug in my hair?"

Joy laughed, relieved at Sabrina's joking.

"How do you feel?" Amanda asked.

"All right. They have me on antibiotics."

Amanda stepped closer. "That's not unusual."

Sabrina yawned and then said, "I'm so ready to get out of here."

"Of course you are," Joy said.

Five minutes later, Joy left, leaving Amanda to speak with the nurse after the shift change. As she stepped out of the room, she collided with Sassie. The woman brushed her eyes as she stepped away from Joy.

Joy asked, "Did I hurt you?"

"I'm fine," Sassie said. "Sorry. I wasn't paying attention." Her eyes were red and her face blotchy. She stood straight. "I had an update from Rebekah."

Joy eagerly asked, "And?"

"Nothing. They have no leads on who took the safe." Sassie met Joy's gaze. "How about you? Have you found anything about who hit Sabrina?"

Joy shook her head. "I don't have any leads either. I wouldn't say we've hit a dead end. Hopefully just a roundabout."

Sassie looked as if she might cry.

Joy reached out and touched her arm. "Are you sure you're all right?"

"I'm fine." Sassie wrapped her arms around herself. "Have you ever done something so foolish you don't know how to fix it?"

Joy couldn't think of anything off the top of her head, but she was sure there was something. "What did you do?" she asked.

"Something a long time ago. I had no idea what the consequences would be."

Joy waited.

"Do you think there's a way to salvage those mistakes we make?"

"Yes," Joy said. "Of course. Nothing is irredeemable."

"What would *you* do?" Sassie asked. "If you'd made a horrible mistake years ago?"

Joy answered, "I'd talk it out with the people involved."

Sassie shook her head. "This is beyond talking out.... It's gone on too long." She sighed.

"Does this have to do with Bob? And the missing safe?"

Sassie hesitated and then shook her head. "How is Sabrina?"

"She's on antibiotics. But she seems to be doing all right." Joy glanced down the hall. "How's Bob?"

Sassie shrugged. "The same. Maybe a little worse."

"I'm sorry," Joy said.

"So am I." Sassie sighed again and then hurried to the elevator.

Just after Joy opened the gift shop, Evelyn stepped inside, her empty coffee cup in her hand.

She asked, "How is Sabrina?"

Joy gave her an update.

"When you see her again, tell her I'm praying for her."

"I will," Joy answered.

Evelyn held up her empty cup.

Joy smiled and pointed to the full pot of coffee. "Help yourself."

"How are you doing?" Evelyn asked as Joy followed her to the back counter.

"Worried about Sabrina. And about something else…"

Evelyn stopped just before reaching the counter and turned around. "What's going on?"

Joy had always been reserved when it came to talking about her marriage or any family problems, but she had to tell someone—besides her lawyer and accountant. She explained the accusation against Wilson.

"That's awful." Evelyn put her mug on the counter. "I'm so sorry you have to deal with this at the same time as Sabrina's accident."

A lump quickly lodged in Joy's throat and tears filled her eyes. Evelyn drew Joy into a hug just as Joy's phone rang. She pulled away and dug her phone out of her pocket. *Carlos.* "It's my lawyer," she said to Evelyn.

"You should take it." Evelyn said. "I'll see you later."

Joy accepted the call.

Carlos jumped right into the topic at hand. "The documents from 2012 and 2014 are missing from Daybreak's files too."

"Their hard files?" Joy asked.

"No, their electronic files. They don't have hard copies. Someone broke into the system and deleted the information from Wilson's accounts for those years."

"Why didn't you tell me that before I scanned all those files in the middle of the night?" Joy asked.

"Sorry."

"Can't they determine who deleted the files?"

Evelyn held up her cup of coffee and waved at Joy.

Joy waved back.

Carlos answered, "The log-in record shows it was Wilson."

Joy gasped. "No."

"I'm afraid so," Carlos said.

"Who told you that?"

"The Daybreak attorney."

"Someone set Wilson up."

"There's no evidence to indicate that. The missing chunks of money disappeared in 2012 and 2014."

"How much money are we talking about?"

"Five hundred thousand each year."

Joy felt sick. "They think Wilson stole a million dollars?"

"That's right," Carlos said.

Joy's voice shook as she spoke. "I know my husband wasn't a crook. We need to prove him innocent."

"What ideas do you have?" Carlos asked.

"I'm not sure yet, but I'll come up with something. And I need you not to believe everything Daybreak tells you. This isn't right."

"Okay," Carlos said. "Let me know when you come up with something."

"I will," Joy said. "I promise."

"In the meantime, Daybreak would like to see your tax records for 2012 and 2014 and your checking and savings accounts records."

Joy shook her head even though Carlos couldn't see her. "I'm not sure Wilson saved records for more than five years or so. I'll ask Randi if she saves them for longer."

"You can see if your bank will access your checking and savings records."

Joy sighed. "Not without a subpoena."

"All right," Carlos said. "I'll let them know. They typically only save records for seven years, so the company may be out of luck there too."

Joy ended the call. She was tempted to contact one of Wilson's colleagues at Daybreak but knew she shouldn't. Could she trust any of their employees? She wasn't even certain who was still there. Surely some had retired. Others may have moved on.

She left a message for her accountant and then poured herself another cup of coffee, feeling torn between finding out who hit Sabrina and who was trying to frame Wilson. The two people she held most dear, the two people she respected the most.

She didn't want to tell Sabrina what was going on as far as the accusations against her father. That would crush her. She couldn't tell her now.

Who could she talk to about the accusations against Wilson? She knew Evelyn or Anne would listen, but they never knew Wilson. They had no idea of his integrity and honesty.

Hope. That was who she could talk it through with. She'd known and loved Wilson. She might even have an idea of what Joy could do to prove him innocent.

She texted her sister. Sabrina is running a fever but doing all right. I've had something unrelated to her come up. Could you call me when you get a chance?

And then she waited.

Hope didn't call her, but Randi did. She got right to the point. "I only keep records for five years. I'm so sorry—I don't have yours that far back."

Joy thanked her and hung up.

Then Evelyn called. "How about lunch?"

"I'll check in with Sabrina and let you know," Joy answered. But then a customer came in and then another. Joy sold two more Father's Day cards and a Get Well card and prayed three more blessings.

Just as Joy finally had a chance to text Sabrina, Rob came into the shop.

He gave a half-hearted smile. "Do you have any flowers for sale?"

"Absolutely," Joy said. "What do you have in mind?"

"Daisies? Lilies? Roses?" He shook his head. "I'm not feeling very decisive."

"How are you?" Joy asked, growing concerned.

"Weirdly exhausted."

"I wouldn't say *weirdly*," Joy answered. "You have good reason to be exhausted. You've been taking care of Sabrina and the girls, all while battling fears about Sabrina's health."

Rob turned to the flower case and pointed to a vase of pink roses. "I think Sabrina would like those."

"I do too." Joy stepped to the case and pulled out the vase. "How about a pink-and-white polka-dot bow?"

"Perfect," Rob said.

As Joy tied the bow, Rob leaned against the counter.

"How were the girls last night?" Joy asked. "Did they stay in bed?"

He nodded. "I was up late answering work emails."

"How about a cup of coffee?" Joy pointed to the coffeepot on the counter behind him.

"That would be great."

"Grab a cup and lid from the cupboard."

After Rob returned, cradling the cup of coffee in both hands, his expression became even more serious. "Sabrina said they put her on antibiotics."

Joy finished tying the bow on the vase. "They did. I saw her this morning before work."

"How did she seem?"

"All right," Joy answered. "Amanda said running a fever isn't unusual."

"That's what Sabrina said." Rob took a sip of coffee and then said, "Each day Sabrina is worse. At first it seemed like this might not be a big deal, just a night in the hospital. Then we waited. Yesterday, I felt better, knowing the surgery had gone well. But this morning I feel scared again."

Joy stepped out from behind the counter and gave Rob a gentle hug, careful not to jar him and cause him to spill his coffee. "This is a big deal."

He hugged her back as well as he could with one arm. "I keep thinking about you when Wilson died. You went through this, except worse."

Joy hugged him a little tighter. "Sabrina is going to be all right. I'm sure of it."

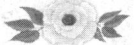

About five minutes after Rob left, Lacy started her shift. A few minutes later, Hope hurried into the gift shop. "I had a meeting at the main campus," she said. "I thought I'd stop by to see what you needed."

"Do you have a few minutes to talk?" Joy asked.

Hope nodded and followed Joy into the back room.

After Joy told her about the accusations against Wilson, Hope shook her head. "That's horrible."

"I know," Joy said.

"You have to stop this."

"I'm trying." Joy pushed her hair back from her face. "I feel overwhelmed with it all. Do you have any ideas of how I can prove him innocent?"

"Have you made a list? Broken down what you know and what you can do and can't do, concerning each category?"

Joy shook her head. "I've been taking notes but that's it."

"Come on." Hope smiled encouragingly. "You're the queen of lists."

Hope was right. Joy had been too overwhelmed to remember her usual method. She dug her notebook out of her purse. Then she grabbed a pen from her desktop.

She opened the notebook and wrote down five categories at the top of the page: *Sabrina's health, hit-and-run driver, safe thief, Hannah* "*poisoned*," and *accusations against Wilson*. Sabrina and Wilson were most important, as always. It would be icing on the cake if she could figure out who the safe thief was and what happened to Hannah. She looked up at her sister. "I'll fill in each category as the day goes on." She closed the notebook. "Thank you for the reminder."

Hope smiled again. "Call if you want to talk anything through. I don't have any meetings this afternoon." She held up her phone. "I was going to go see Sabrina, but Rob said she's sleeping. I don't want to wake her."

Joy understood. That was how she felt too.

After Hope left, Joy buckled down to get caught up on her work to-do list. Just starting a chart with all the concerns swirling around in her head helped. She wasn't worrying quite so much. At eleven thirty she had a text from Evelyn. CAN YOU DO LUNCH WITH ANNE AND ME AND SHIRLEY? IN FIFTEEN MINUTES.

Joy texted Rob, asking if he wanted her to come sit with Sabrina on her lunch break.

NO, he texted back. SHE'S STILL SLEEPING, AND I'M GETTING QUITE A BIT OF WORK DONE AS I SIT HERE. I'LL TEXT YOU IF SHE WAKES UP.

Joy texted Evelyn back. MEET YOU IN THE GROVE AT 11:45. PUT ON YOUR THINKING CAP. I NEED HELP!

Sassie only had just over a week until her grand reopening. If the rumor around town was that she'd poisoned Hannah, would anyone show up for it? Joy still didn't have any idea if Sassie was innocent or not, but if she was, Joy wanted it known. If she was in fact innocent, Joy wanted Sassie to be exonerated as much as she wanted Wilson to be. The accusations against Wilson didn't hurt him—only his reputation. But the accusations against Sassie could do lasting damage.

Joy arrived in the Grove with her sandwich, along with her water bottle. She'd had enough coffee for the day—her anxiety wasn't going to get any better if she kept feeding it caffeine.

Evelyn, Anne, and Shirley already had a table in the corner. As Joy approached, they all rose to give her a hug.

Joy treasured these women. What a blessing it was to have them as her best friends in her new life in Charleston.

"Any word on Sabrina?" Anne asked.

Joy shook her head. "I just texted with Rob. She's still running a fever. She's sleeping now. If she wakes up, he's going to text me."

Joy put her lunch bag and water bottle on the table and then pulled her notebook from her bag. "Sabrina and her family are my front burner, but the whole mystery with Sassie and Hannah and the missing safe and who hit Sabrina is simmering too. And then, yesterday, I had a phone call about Wilson."

"Wilson?" Shirley asked.

"Yes," Joy said. "I already told Evelyn about this, but Shirley and Anne, I need to tell you too." In a shaky voice she explained what was going on.

"How odd," Anne said.

Shirley agreed.

"Right?" Joy sighed. "When it rains it pours." She motioned to her notebook. "But enough about that. Besides proving Wilson innocent, my top priority is to find out who hit Sabrina and then fled the scene. But I think I may need to do something else first. Can y'all help me solve the Sassie Crane mystery?"

Her three friends nodded.

"Sassie's finishing a big expansion of her spa and has the reopening celebration coming up. I'm afraid she might be innocent, even though she acts guilty, and her entire business might tank. That wouldn't be fair." Joy thought of Wilson being innocent but accused of embezzling money. The same could be true of Sassie—she could be innocent even though she appeared guilty. "I'm hoping that by figuring out what's going on with Sassie and her business, I can discover who stole the safe and hit Sabrina."

Joy updated Evelyn and Anne about Cowboy Bob and what Sassie said that morning. "She regrets some choice she made years ago. I wonder if there's a connection between that and what's happening now."

Evelyn took out her phone. "That's interesting that she'd say that. I did more research on Riley."

"Oh?" Joy had been thinking about him too.

Evelyn turned her phone around. A photo on her screen showed five people, two young women with big hair and three young men. "This is from the Peninsula High yearbook when they were all seniors." She pointed at a young woman. "Hannah O'Connor."

Joy peered at the screen. The girl looked like Hannah.

"Parker Hollingsworth. Ernest Crane. Sassie Crane. And Riley O'Connor."

"Riley O'Connor?" Joy gasped. "Is he related to Hannah?"

Evelyn nodded. "He's her brother." She put her phone down.

Joy's mouth dropped open. "But Sassie claimed to barely remember him."

"There's no way Sassie wouldn't remember him. She went to high school with him. He was Sassie's best friend's brother. I searched through several yearbooks. Riley was a grade ahead and then was held back a year, so he and Hannah were in the same grade by the time they were sophomores," Evelyn continued. "Riley was poisoned in 1987. He spent three nights in this very hospital and then he seems to have completely disappeared. A week later Ernest was arrested. All of that was in the newspaper."

A shiver shot up Joy's spine. "Do you think Riley was murdered?"

"I have no idea," Evelyn said. "I don't remember a big search or anything. I'm guessing he left town of his own accord. But speaking of Riley, I solved the mystery of Sassie's given name—I think—and it also led me to Riley O'Connor."

"How so?"

"According to vital records, Sassie's paternal grandmother's name was Sarah Marie Houston Crane. I tried Sarah Marie Crane and came across a 1966 birth certificate. And then a 1987 marriage certificate."

"Really?"

"Yes. To Riley O'Connor."

"Wow." Joy leaned forward. "And to think Sassie said she didn't remember him." She shook her head. "Any other vital records?"

"No." Evelyn shrugged. "There's no divorce certificate. No death certificate for Riley. Nothing."

Joy picked up her sandwich. "So, apparently, Sassie changed her name from Sarah to Sassie after her marriage, in 1987, and before Ashley was born in 1988?"

Evelyn nodded. "I found one more thing."

"What's that?" Joy asked.

"Sassie reported an antique safe stolen from her salon the day before Ernest was arrested. The safe belonged to her grandfather."

"What was in the safe?" Shirley asked.

"That wasn't disclosed," Evelyn said.

Anne said, "The Cranes went to St. Michael's. Sassie and Ashley still go there."

"Do you remember anything about the family?"

Anne took a sip of her tea. "I remember when Ernest came home to Charleston after being away—"

"In prison?" Joy asked.

"Yes," Anne said. "Although I don't think he came directly to Charleston after being released. No one in the family talked about him, but others did. He attended services a few times, and I remember meeting him. He kept his head down and didn't say much." Anne paused a moment and then said, "Granddaddy Crane and Sassie fascinated me, along with Ashley. That's probably why I remember this."

"What do you remember?" Joy asked.

"That Ernest had gone to prison for running a chop shop ring out of his auto body shop."

"That's what Evelyn said earlier. He ran it out of the Crane Building," Joy said.

Anne nodded. "And the bulk of the money from his crimes was never recovered. Supposedly there was an accusation against Sassie that she was helping Ernest. The rumor was that Sassie testified against him in a plea deal."

Joy tapped her pen on the table. "So thirty-five years ago, a safe was stolen from Sassie's shop, and then Riley was poisoned, and then, according to a rumor, Sassie struck a plea deal and Ernest was arrested? Do you think Ernest's chop shop money was in the safe?"

Evelyn shrugged. "If it was, who do you think ended up with the money?"

"Maybe it was still in the safe all these years later," Joy said. "Maybe that's why it was stolen. Maybe that's why Ernest returned to Charleston—to steal the safe."

"And set Sassie up as trying to poison Hannah to ruin her business for revenge?" Anne asked.

"Perhaps..." If so, did Ernest hit Sabrina too? Was he responsible for everything that happened?

Joy tried to sort through all the information and possibilities of what might have happened on Friday.

And thirty-five years ago.

Riley had been poisoned thirty-five years ago—and now it seemed Hannah might have been poisoned last Friday. The safe had been stolen thirty-five years ago, or so Sassie reported, and now it had been again, last Friday.

Or so Sassie reported.

As she was trying to make sense of all of it, Joy's phone buzzed. It was a text from Rob. S ABRINA'S HAVING A SEIZURE. PLEASE COME.

Chapter Fourteen

As Joy rushed into Sabrina's room, she saw Rob waiting near the back wall. Nurses stood on each side of the bed as if standing guard. Sabrina had an oxygen mask over her face.

Rob reached for Joy's hand. "The seizure stopped a minute ago. It seemed like it lasted forever."

Joy imagined it did feel that way. She squeezed his hand, as much to comfort him as to strengthen herself.

One of the nurses said, "I'll go call the doctor."

Another nurse said, "I'll stay here."

Joy leaned toward Rob and whispered, "Did they tell you to stay back here?"

"Yes," he whispered.

Sabrina began to stir. Then she opened her eyes and looked at the nurse.

"You had a seizure," the nurse said. "But you're all right now."

Sabrina asked, "Where's Rob?"

"Right here," he said. "Your mom is here too."

"What happened?" Sabrina asked.

The nurse motioned for Rob and Joy to move up to the bed. They did, standing on each side as the nurse stepped to the computer.

Sabrina reached for Rob with her left hand and Joy with her right and then she began to cry.

Joy thought her heart might break. Again she remembered Wilson, but quickly pushed the reminder away. Joy turned to the nurse. "Is it normal to have a seizure after brain surgery?"

"It happens," the nurse answered. "We'll see what the doctor says. He may prescribe something. How's your pain?"

"A six."

"It's time for more medication," the nurse said.

Before long, Sabrina closed her eyes and drifted off to sleep. "I can stay so you can go get something to eat," Joy told Rob.

"I'm not hungry." He sat down. "I don't want to go anywhere."

"Okay." Joy glanced at the clock. It was twelve thirty. She had fifteen more minutes until she needed to return to the shop. "I'll go back down. Let me know if you need me."

"I will. Thank you for coming right up." He made eye contact with her. "I was scared."

Joy gave him a hug.

In the elevator, her legs began to shake. When she reached the lobby, Joy ducked into the gift shop. Lacy stood at the counter. One customer, a young woman, looked at the Father's Day cards. Joy said a quick prayer for the woman and her family that the Lord would bless them on Sunday. Then she said a prayer for her family.

Joy stopped at the counter. "I'm going to go for a walk. To clear my head."

"Take your time," Lacy said. "It's been really slow."

On her way out the front door of the hospital with her head down, Joy bumped into someone.

"I'm so sorry," she said as she raised her head.

"Joy." Roger Gaylord smiled down at her as he reached out and touched her arm. "How are you doing? How is Sabrina?"

The warmth of his smile calmed her. "Do you have a minute?"

"Of course," he answered.

"Want to walk with me?"

"Yes," he said.

Roger followed her out the door and then into the shade, next to the building. They walked slowly as Joy told him about the seizure.

"Wow. I'm so sorry."

Tears stung Joy's eyes.

In a voice full of compassion, Roger said, "I'll keep praying for her. And you too."

"Thank you," Joy said. "I really appreciate it."

They continued around the hospital, talking as they walked.

"How are your granddaughters doing?"

Joy explained that Eloise seemed to be having a harder time than Mallory. "She felt the hit-and-run was her fault because she'd delayed Sabrina from leaving the house. I explained that it wasn't her fault—it was entirely the fault of the driver."

Roger exhaled. "That's so good that she could tell you how she was feeling. Imagine if she hadn't been able to."

Joy agreed.

When they arrived back at the front entrance, Roger said, "I have a meeting with Garrison in a few minutes, but I'm so glad we bumped into each other."

"So am I," Joy said. She felt more settled pouring her heart out to him, but she still felt the need to keep walking and burn off some nervous energy. He stepped back toward the hospital, giving her a wave as he did. He was a good man.

She crossed the street and headed alongside the Crane Building, aiming for the waterfront.

As she neared the entrance of Sassie's Hair and Spa, she heard someone shout, "I don't know who to believe anymore. Why did you wait so long to come see me on Friday?"

Joy squinted. Sassie stepped out the front door of the salon and held the door wide open. She said something, but so quietly Joy couldn't hear her.

Several people stopped on the sidewalk and stared.

Joy sped up.

"Hannah," Sassie said. "Come inside."

As Joy reached the shop, she could see Hannah standing under the awning. "Sassie! Hannah! Hello!"

Sassie shaded her eyes and then smiled. "Joy! So nice to see you."

As Joy approached, she asked, "Is everyone doing okay?" She smiled at Hannah.

Hannah frowned.

Sassie stepped back into the shop. Joy waited until Hannah followed Sassie, and then she stepped in and closed the door.

Ashley stood at the counter with a pasted-on smile on her face.

Hannah stopped in the hallway door and turned to Joy, although Sassie continued into the pedicure room.

"How are you feeling?" Joy asked.

"Better." Hannah pushed her hair up in the back. "I had my doctor's appointment this morning. He ordered more tests. And Sassie just trimmed my hair." Hannah frowned. "But then she offered me a pedicure and massage, and I'm beginning to wonder if maybe Parker is right after all."

"What do you mean?"

"If Sassie didn't do anything, why is she being so generous?"

"Hannah," Ashley said, "it was my idea. It's called customer service. You had a bad experience here Friday. We're just trying to make being here pleasant for you again."

Hannah scowled.

"Mother didn't do anything to you," Ashley said. "Go enjoy your pedicure and massage. I doubt if Mother will offer you anything free again."

Sassie came back down the hall and offered her hand—plus a smile—to Hannah, who hesitated for a moment. But then she walked with her out of the room.

After the pedicure door closed, Joy whispered, "What was that all about?"

Ashley sighed. "It looks like Parker's accusations are affecting Hannah."

Before Joy could respond, the front door opened and Rebekah stepped inside. "Hello, Ashley. Hello, Joy."

"Hi, Rebekah," Joy replied. "Any progress on finding the driver who hit Sabrina?"

Rebekah shook her head. "I'll keep working on it."

Joy's face grew warm. She respected Rebekah, but Joy feared she wasn't doing all she could. She also guessed most family members of victims felt the same way.

Rebekah looked at Ashley. "Is your mother around? I have some information for her. About a break-in early Friday morning."

More than anything at the moment, Joy wanted to stick around and hear what Rebekah had to say, but she wasn't sure she could get away with it. Thankfully, Sassie, who overheard Rebekah as she stepped into the lobby, made it possible.

"Let's go into my office," Sassie said to Rebekah. "And I'd like Joy to come with us."

Ashley gave her mother a puzzled look.

"I need you out here," Sassie said. "Joy will take notes, right? We'll tell you what Rebekah says."

Joy nodded, glad she had her bag with her notebook in it. Sassie motioned for both Rebekah and Joy to follow her to the hallway. They passed the pedicure room and the manicure room. Then the massage area and the facial area. "These will all be moved to the new spa space," Sassie said. "Then we'll expand this room for a bigger hair salon."

At the end of the hall was Sassie's office. It was small and cramped with a desk, an office chair, two straight-backed chairs, and a bookcase full of binders and books. There was a photograph of Ashley and Lindsay on the desk, but that was the only picture. There was no art in the room. A closed laptop sat on the desk.

"Please, sit down." Sassie lowered herself into the office chair.

Joy sat and took her notebook from her bag. After Rebekah settled in her chair, she took an electronic tablet from her bag. "We found some security tape from the insurance office across the street. They have a camera pointed at their door with a view of your warehouse door too. It looks as if someone broke into the warehouse around three o'clock Friday morning."

"Do you think the safe was stolen then?" Sassie asked.

Rebekah shook her head. "When the person left they didn't have anything visible with them. Certainly not anything as big as a safe."

"Do you have video from Friday afternoon from the same place showing if the safe was stolen then?"

Rebekah shook her head again. "The doorway to your warehouse was blocked by the SUV." She turned on her tablet. "I'm hoping you can identify the person who broke in early Friday morning. I've blown up the still shots." Rebekah put her tablet on the desk.

Sassie's face froze.

"What is it?" Rebekah asked.

Joy stood and stepped to the side of the desk so she could see the photo. She gasped.

"Do you recognize him?" Rebekah asked.

Sassie didn't answer.

But Joy did. "It's Cowboy Bob."

Rebekah and Joy walked out to the lobby while Sassie stayed in her office with the door closed.

"What's going on?" Ashley asked.

Joy glanced at Rebekah, who shrugged.

"Your mother wanted some time alone," Joy finally said.

"Why?"

Rebekah hesitated and then said, "We have security footage of a man breaking into the warehouse side of this building early Friday morning."

"Oh?" Ashley's voice was low. "Did Mother recognize him?"

Rebekah glanced at Joy again.

Joy leaned toward Ashley. "It was Cowboy Bob."

"Cowboy Bob? But he's ill, right? I thought he doesn't have much time to live."

"It was definitely him," Joy said. "No doubt. He even had his cowboy hat on."

"Maybe someone was posing as him, wearing a cowboy hat. Wasn't he already in the hospital?"

Joy thought for a moment. "I think he said he was admitted early Friday morning. The break-in was at 3:36, so he could have been admitted after that."

"Does Cowboy Bob have a last name?" Rebekah asked.

Joy had to think for a moment and then it came to her. "Chorro. Robert Chorro. He lives in Montana."

Rebekah asked, "Any idea where in Montana?"

"All I know is that he works on a ranch." Joy rubbed the side of her face. "He was still in the hospital this morning. Room 417."

Rebekah stood. "I'd like to know why Sassie won't speak with me."

"Welcome to the club." Ashley shrugged. "The good news is she can't stay in her office forever."

"I need to get on with the investigation," Rebekah said. "I'll go speak with Mr. Chorro."

Joy stood. "I'll walk to the hospital with you."

They both told Ashley goodbye. As they crossed the street to the hospital, Rebekah asked, "Would you go up to Mr. Chorro's room and introduce me?"

"Yes," Joy said. Lacy had two more hours of work in the gift shop. She had time. As they walked through the lobby, Joy said,

"Would you mind if Evelyn comes with us? She knew Sassie and her group of friends when they were all in high school. She might have some thoughts after meeting Bob."

"That would be fine," Rebekah said. "As long as she can go now. I don't have much time."

They stopped in at the records department, and Joy quickly explained their mission to Evelyn.

"I was just about ready to take a break." Evelyn stood. "I'll go up with you."

When they reached Cowboy Bob's room, Joy knocked on the door. "It's me, Joy. I met you Saturday and then saw you on Sunday with Ashley."

"Oh. Hello, Joy. Come on in." Bob sat up in bed, his hat on, looking even more gaunt than he had two days before.

Joy stepped forward. "I have two friends with me." She gestured to Evelyn first. "Evelyn Perry, who works here at the hospital. And Detective Osborne." She gestured to Rebekah. "She's a detective with the Charleston Police Department."

Bob took his hat off, showing a buzz cut. "Oh?"

Rebekah nodded. "I have a few questions for you."

"All right."

She took her tablet from her bag and held it up so he could see it. "Can you tell me about this photograph?"

He squinted at the image and then motioned for her to move it closer. She handed it to him. He held it up and squinted even more.

"What can you tell me?" Rebekah asked.

"Nothing." He handed her the tablet. "Not until I speak with a lawyer."

Chapter Fifteen

Rebekah walked ahead to the waiting room with Evelyn and Joy following her. When they all stopped, Joy asked Evelyn if Bob looked familiar.

"Honestly, no. Not at all. But he appears to be quite ill."

Rebekah agreed.

"All right." Joy pointed down the hall. "I'm going to go back and check on Sabrina. I'll see both of you soon."

Rebekah and Evelyn headed to the elevator while Joy walked to Sabrina's room. She peered inside. Rob had his head down, staring at his closed laptop. Sabrina was turned toward him, on her side, the bandaged part of her head showing. Her eyes were open, but she was staring into space.

Joy slipped away without disturbing them, deciding to take the stairs instead of the elevator. She stopped in the stairwell when she reached the lobby floor and sat down on the bottom step. She had no control over what happened to Sabrina. She had to trust God with her daughter. She had no other choice. There was nothing she could do.

But there was something she could do as far as Wilson being accused of embezzling. She'd do whatever necessary to defend and protect his good name. Even if it meant going to Houston herself—although she'd need to wait until Sabrina was on the mend.

"Joy?"

She rose and turned around. Ralph, Anne's husband and the hospital chaplain, stood on the step above her.

"Are you all right?" he asked.

"Yes," Joy said. "But could you check in with Sabrina and Rob when you have a chance? She's in 413. I think it would bring comfort to them if you would pray with them." It would bring comfort to Joy too.

Lacy went home at two, leaving Joy to wait on customers for the next hour until the gift shop closed. Had her experience at the hospital in Houston when Wilson died influenced her to take the job at Mercy Hospital? Had sharing that experience with Amanda caused her to recommend Joy for the job?

Less than a year later, Amanda had called her about the position at Mercy in Charleston. Joy toyed with the idea of relocating, longing to be closer to Sabrina and her family. Wilson had left her well cared for, but she struggled with how she would spend her time if she moved. Sure, she could volunteer. And she'd enjoy as many get-togethers with her granddaughters as possible. But she didn't want to be too dependent on Sabrina. Perhaps, someday, she would be forced to be dependent on her daughter, but she wanted to be as independent as possible until that time came.

Having a job with responsibilities and colleagues and built-in relationships seemed to be the healthiest possibility for Joy. When Amanda called about the position, Joy asked if she'd spoken with Sabrina about it. "Of course," she said. "We all think it's a brilliant idea."

And it was. Sabrina convinced her to put her house on the market in Houston as soon as possible, saying if she didn't get that job another one would come open. But she did get the job, and the house sold immediately. Everything fell into place at just the right time. God clearly had His hand in her move to Charleston.

An unexpected blessing was how much her being in Charleston helped Eloise. She'd been devastated by her pappy's death. She'd had a deep relationship with her grandfather. Mallory did too, but she didn't understood how permanent death was, and because of that she'd seemed to slowly accept the reality that Pappy wasn't coming back. It had hit Eloise all at once—the day they'd buried Wilson.

That was what Joy thought about as she turned the sign to closed on the door to the shop. Then she retreated to her office and googled *Robert Chorro, Montana*. He worked on a ranch near Missoula. She couldn't locate any details as far as a wife or children. He had no criminal history. She first found information for him from 1995, when he was listed as working as a clown at a rodeo. She couldn't find a record of his birth or a record of his family in Montana—or in South Carolina.

Who was Robert Chorro, and where had he come from?

A half hour later, after she'd seen to all the closing tasks, she locked the gift shop door and stepped into the lobby.

Sitting in the middle, in the circle of chairs under the chandelier, was a bald-headed man wearing jeans and a black T-shirt. It was the same man she'd seen in the elevator. He was the one who'd asked if she was all right after she'd found out Wilson was being accused of embezzling money and that Sabrina needed brain surgery.

Desperate to find out who hit Sabrina, Joy sat down in the chair beside him. "Hello," she said.

The man nodded, acknowledging her.

"I wanted to thank you for being so kind to me in the elevator the other day." She extended her hand, and he shook it. She continued, "My name is Joy Atkins. I manage the gift shop here, but my daughter is a patient on the fourth floor. It's been a hard week."

He gave her a faint smile.

"Do you mind if I ask you a few questions?"

He cocked his head. "Depends on the questions."

She smiled. "How about if I ask and then you decide?"

"All right."

"I wouldn't be so intrusive normally, but my daughter—my only child—was in a hit-and-run incident on Friday. She was riding her bike, and the driver of a black SUV hit her. She has a head injury and is still in the hospital. So far there's no information as to who was driving."

"I'm so sorry," he said.

"Thank you." Joy smiled. "I believe I've seen you a few different times over the last five days. Did I see you here in the lobby last Friday morning?"

He shrugged.

"Then at Sassie's Salon and Spa last Friday afternoon."

His face reddened.

"The last time was in the elevator."

"I do remember seeing you in the elevator," he said with a slight Southern accent. "I was visiting a friend on the fourth floor."

"Bob Chorro?"

He hesitated and then answered, "Yes, ma'am."

"Are you from Montana?"

His dark eyes sparkled. "No, ma'am. We were friends when we were younger, here in Charleston. I haven't seen him in years."

"Any chance you're Ernest Crane?"

He leaned back in his chair. "Is it that obvious?"

"Were you hoping no one would recognize you?"

He shrugged. "I've learned not to hope for much."

"But you've tried to disguise your looks throughout the last five days."

He shrugged again.

"Why?"

"I was playing different roles," he said. "On Friday morning I was the friend visiting Bob, although he was asleep and I lost my nerve and didn't wake him. On Friday afternoon, I posed as a beauty product rep so I could hopefully see Sassie."

"Have you seen her?" Joy asked.

"No, ma'am," Ernest said. "I've pretty much failed when it comes to Sassie for the last thirty-five years."

"Were you looking for the safe?"

He whistled. "You don't let up, do you?"

She forced herself not to apologize. Perhaps she was finally making progress in finding the driver who hit Sabrina. "Were you looking for the safe?" she repeated.

"No," he said. "I figured that safe was long gone. Honestly, I was flabbergasted to hear it was stolen Friday afternoon, right after I stopped by the shop." He inhaled deeply and then exhaled slowly. "I really was looking for Sassie."

"Why?"

"I have some business with her, concerning our grandfather's will." He met Joy's gaze with intensity. "Please don't ask me any more questions about that."

Joy scooted forward in her chair. "Where are you staying?"

Ernest shook his head. "Here and there."

"How long will you be in Charleston?"

"At least until I can talk with Sassie."

"You said Bob was asleep when you tried to see him before. Have you tried to see him since then?"

Ernest's eyes grew misty.

"Any chance Bob used another name when he was younger?"

"I'm going to plead the fifth on that question too."

"Fair enough." Joy extended her hand again. "I'm pleased to meet you, Ernest Crane."

He shook her hand. "I'm pleased to meet you too."

"Hopefully I'll see you around."

Ernest sighed. "We'll see."

Joy stood, waved, and then continued on. Ernest Crane wasn't the boogeyman she'd expected him to be.

As she reached the elevator, the doors opened and Anne appeared. She gave Joy a hug.

"Do you have a minute?" Joy asked.

"Absolutely," Anne answered.

Joy told her Ernest Crane was sitting in the lobby.

"Really?"

"He seems troubled. Maybe he'll remember you from St. Michael's."

"I doubt it," Anne said. "But I'd like to meet him again."

The two walked back to the center of the lobby. Ernest sat in the chair, staring at the floor. Joy approached, clearing her throat. "Ernest."

He lifted his head.

"This is my friend Anne Mabry. Her husband was the pastor at St. Michael's."

He quickly stood and extended his hand. "It's nice to meet you, ma'am."

"We met years ago," Anne said. "At church."

"I attended St. Michael's as a child," he said. "And I did go back a few times. People were always nice to me there."

"That's good to know," Anne said. "My husband retired a few years ago. He's a chaplain now at the hospital if you need someone to talk with."

"Thank you, ma'am," he said.

Anne took a card from her pocket. "All of his information is here. Just call him. He'll meet you anywhere in the hospital or you can go to his office."

"I appreciate it." Ernest took the card and then looked toward the exit. "I need to get going, but thank you, ladies."

Joy and Anne both watched Ernest as he made his way to the sliding doors. His shoulders were stooped a little. He seemed to be carrying a heavy load.

Joy told Anne goodbye and then headed for the fourth floor. As she stepped off the elevator, she saw a cowboy hat on someone sitting on a chair in the waiting area.

As she passed by, she turned. Cowboy Bob. He was dressed in jeans, a short-sleeve forest-green shirt, and cowboy boots. She stopped. "What are you doing?" she asked.

"Resting," he said.

"Where are you headed?"

"Over to speak with Sassie." He sighed. "I'm hoping she has a recommendation for an attorney. I had one here, but he's long gone. Passed away twenty years ago, according to the receptionist at the firm he worked for."

"Could someone else at the firm take you on?" Joy asked.

Bob shrugged. "I need to talk with Sassie." He scooted up to the edge of the chair, leaned on his cane, and then stood.

"I can walk with you."

Joy was afraid he might not make it on his own.

Bob swayed as he spoke. "Oh, there's no need for that."

Joy grabbed his arm. "Humor me."

He grinned. "Are you going to call your detective friend?"

"No." Joy smiled. "At least not at the moment." She linked her arm through his free arm, and they began plodding toward the elevator. They rode down with someone coming from the fifth floor and didn't talk.

Once they reached the lobby, as she and Bob shuffled along, he asked, "How is your daughter doing?"

She hadn't said a word to him about Sabrina. "How do you know about my daughter?"

"Oh, I've been talking with her husband. With Rob. He says you're the best mother-in-law ever."

Joy couldn't help but smile. "I didn't think I could appreciate Rob any more than I already did—until this very moment."

"He's a good kid," Bob said. "A good husband and father, right?"

"The best," Joy replied. "How about you? Do you have a wife? Any children?"

He hesitated before saying, "That's a complicated question for me."

Joy cringed. She wasn't usually so forthright. "Does that translate into 'That's a nosy question'?"

"Not at all." A hint of a Southern accent could be detected in his voice. Perhaps spending time in Charleston was reviving it.

Joy waited for Bob to further respond to her question, since he deemed it not to be nosy, but he didn't. They'd reached the hospital exit and passed through. The afternoon had grown overcast, and the humidity was high. Bob concentrated on walking. With each step, his weight on Joy's arm grew greater.

As did the weight of Joy's questions.

"Do you know anything about Riley O'Connor?" Joy asked, helping Bob step off the curb as the walk signal changed.

"Who?"

"Riley O'Connor. He lived in Charleston back in the 1980s."

Bob didn't answer.

"How about Hannah O'Connor?" Joy asked.

Bob slowed, nearly stopping in the middle of the street. Joy urged him on.

He asked her, "What do you know about Hannah?"

"I met her for the first time on Friday. She's a friend of Sassie's—and a client of hers."

"Tell me more about her," Bob said.

"She's married to Parker Hollingsworth. They have a daughter, Lindsay."

"A daughter?"

"Yes," Joy answered. "She's seventeen."

As they reached the curb, Bob asked, "Hannah must have been an older mom."

"So you do remember Hannah?" Joy asked.

Bob didn't answer.

"She must have had Lindsay when she was around forty. Not exactly young."

"What's Parker like?"

"I'm not sure," Joy answered. "He seems nice enough."

"Good to Hannah?"

Joy shrugged as she led Bob to the curb and pushed the walk button. "You haven't answered my question about Riley O'Connor."

"I'm working on it," he said and then fell silent.

After they'd crossed the second street, Joy said, "I'm surprised the doctor released you."

"Oh, he didn't," he said. "I checked myself out."

"Against medical advice? Why would you do that?"

He sighed. "I wasn't getting any better. Why should I stay? If you were dying from kidney cancer, would you want to spend the time you had left wearing a hospital gown?"

Joy tightened her grip on his arm. "I guess not."

When they were a half block from the salon, the door opened and Hannah exited, turning the other direction without seeing Joy. Joy wanted to call out to her, to see if she recognized Bob, but Hannah was moving quickly. Shirley came out behind her. She turned to Joy and Bob.

She beamed when she saw Joy. "Hello! Who do you have with you?"

Joy introduced Bob to Shirley and then asked, "What have you been up to?"

Shirley held up both hands. "A manicure." She wiggled her fingers, the orange polish sparkling on her nails.

"Nice." Joy smiled.

Shirley held the door, and Joy helped Bob up the step and into the shop. As they passed by, Shirley whispered, "I can stick around. It looks like you might need some help."

"Thank you," Joy whispered back. "I need to get back to Sabrina."

"Hello, Bob." Ashley stood at the counter with a smile on her face. "Look at you. Did you make a break?"

He grinned. "Something like that."

Joy took his arm and propelled him to the first chair.

"Do you want a pedicure?" Ashley asked. "We're having a special."

"I'd love one. It's been years since I've had one." Bob grinned. "But first I need to speak to your mother."

"She's with a client. Can I help you?"

Bob put both hands on his cane and leaned forward. "I don't think so."

Ashley smiled. "Try me?"

He smiled back but didn't say anything more.

"I'll let her know." Ashley headed for the hair cutting room.

"What will you do after you speak to Sassie?" Joy asked Bob.

"Hopefully talk with a lawyer."

"And after that?"

"I have a room at the Dawson Hotel. I'll go back there."

That was a few blocks away. Joy doubted he could walk that far. "How will you get there?"

"I'll call a taxi." His eyes twinkled. "Or order an Uber."

She smiled. Obviously, Cowboy Bob knew how to get around. Maybe she wouldn't need Shirley's help. Joy turned to speak with Shirley, but Shirley was sitting in the chair by the door, texting on her phone. Joy would wait a few more minutes before turning down Shirley's help.

Sassie followed Ashley into the lobby, a concerned expression on her face. "What are you doing out of the hospital?"

Bob pushed up on his cane and said, "I need to speak with an attorney. And then I'm going to talk to Detective Osborne."

Sassie's shoulders slumped. "You promised."

"That was thirty-five years ago. I was young and stupid. Now I'm old and dying. I'm sorry, but I need to do what's right. Better late than never, right?"

Sassie shook her head but said, "Come back into my office. I have an idea."

"You won't change my mind."

"I know," Sassie said. "I don't want to. I just want us to talk things through first."

Chapter Sixteen

AFTER SASSIE AND BOB HEADED down the hall to her office, Joy turned to Ashley. "Are you sure the name Riley O'Connor means nothing to you?"

"Positive."

"What do you know of Hannah's family of origin? Parents? Siblings?"

Ashley tilted her head. "I've never met any of her family. I've met Parker's and saw them at family events—when Lindsay was born and at her birthdays, that sort of thing. They're quiet people—not like Parker at all. I had the impression Hannah's mother had died, but I don't remember hearing anything about a father."

"Did she mention living somewhere besides South Carolina?"

"I think she grew up somewhere else until middle school. Maybe Georgia. Or North Carolina. Somewhere rural." Ashley gave Joy a puzzled look. "Why?"

"Evelyn Perry is a couple of years older than your mother and Hannah, but she seemed to remember that Hannah had a brother—Riley O'Connor."

"Weird," Ashley said. "Sounds like another secret, which is right on par for Mother and the Dare to Dream Team. They should have gone by the Sure to Lie Team instead."

Joy nodded to the hallway where Sassie and Bob had disappeared. "I need to go check on Sabrina, but would you keep me informed?"

"I will," Ashley said. "I'll text you and let you know if anything comes from Mother and Bob's meeting."

Joy didn't mean to upset Ashley, but it couldn't be helped. "Thank you," she said. "And I'll do the same."

Joy turned to Shirley. "It looks like Bob has a plan to get to his hotel. I'm going to head back to the hospital."

"I'll stay a little longer," Shirley said. "Just in case." She lowered her voice. "And I'll see if I can figure out what's going on."

Joy gave her an appreciative smile. Shirley had been listening after all.

Ten minutes later Joy was back in room 413. Sabrina was awake now, and Rob stood beside her bed.

"Hello," Joy said. "How are things going?"

"Better," Sabrina said. "My temperature is normal, and they gave me medication to prevent any more seizures."

"Oh good," Joy said.

Sabrina sighed. "I'm really tired though. More than I was. I think I'm going to try to sleep while Rob gets something to eat."

Joy asked, "Do you need me to go get the girls?"

"No." Rob smiled. "Hope is going to pick them up from Anne's and take them out to dinner, and then I'll meet them at the house at seven. We figured you could use some downtime."

"Oh, I don't know about that," Joy said. But she did need to water her flowers and get some laundry done. "How about if I go to your house and get your laundry? I'll do it with mine and return it tomorrow."

"That would be great," Rob said.

Joy stepped to Sabrina's bed and gave her a kiss on the forehead. "I'll stop by first thing in the morning."

"Thanks. I'm hoping I'll be able to go home tomorrow."

"I hope so too," Joy said.

After walking home to get her car, Joy cut a bouquet of daisies and lilies from her backyard and then drove to Sabrina's house. She decided to do whatever she could so that things would be nice if Sabrina was released the next day. First she let Mopsy out of her crate and out the back door. Then she put the flowers on the dining room table and loaded the dishes from breakfast into the dishwasher. Next she ran the vacuum and stripped and made the beds. She gathered up all the dirty laundry and sheets in two baskets.

After she stowed the baskets in the back of her Mini Cooper, she let Mopsy in and fed her. Then she crated the dog again. She sent Hope a quick text, asking if she and the girls would take Mopsy for a walk when they arrived home.

On her way to her house, Joy passed Sassie's salon. The lights were still on inside. Joy pulled over and checked her phone. She'd forgotten that Ashley was going to text her. Sure enough, she had a text, sent a half hour before. MOTHER'S ATTORNEY FINALLY ARRIVED AND JUST HEADED BACK TO HER OFFICE TO TALK WITH COWBOY BOB, I PRESUME.

Joy texted back. JUST SAW THIS. I WAS AT SABRINA'S TIDYING UP. HOW ARE THINGS GOING?

ARE YOU IN THE NEIGHBORHOOD? BOB IS READY TO TALK, ALTHOUGH MOTHER SAYS HE MAY BE CONFUSED. I TEXTED REBEKAH, BUT IT WOULD HELP ME IF YOU WERE HERE. SHIRLEY HUNG

AROUND—I THINK SHE'S WORRIED ABOUT BOB'S HEALTH. BOB SAID HE DIDN'T RECOGNIZE HER AT FIRST OUT OF HER SCRUBS BUT SHE TOOK CARE OF HIM IN THE ER LAST FRIDAY MORNING.

Joy texted back. I'M CLOSE BY. I CAN BE THERE IN A FEW MINUTES.

THANK YOU, Ashley responded. I'D LIKE TO HAVE YOU LISTENING IN—JUST IN CASE I DON'T REMEMBER THINGS CORRECTLY. THAT WAY MOTHER CAN'T TRY TO CONVINCE ME I HEARD WRONG.

That made Joy sad. SEE YOU IN A FEW MINUTES, she texted. It also made sense that Shirley had taken care of Bob. Shirley couldn't talk about his stay in the ER, but Bob could.

When Joy stepped into the lobby, she found Ashley standing at the counter, Sassie leaning against the wall by the door to the hallway, Shirley in the same chair by the door, and Cowboy Bob and a woman, who appeared to be in her sixties and wore an expensive pants suit, sitting side by side.

Before Joy could say hello to everyone, Sassie asked Ashley, "What is Joy doing here?"

"I asked her to come." Ashley met Joy's gaze and held it.

Joy smiled as she sat down next to Shirley, leaving a space between herself and Cowboy Bob. It didn't bother her that Sassie was so forthright.

The woman stood and stepped toward Joy. "I'm Janet Caltron, Sassie's attorney."

Joy shook her hand. "Hello. I'm Joy Atkins." Before she could say anything else, Rebekah walked into the salon. After she said hello to everyone, she stepped close to Joy.

Joy's hope rose. "Have you made any progress on identifying the driver?"

Rebekah shook her head. "I'm sorry. We still don't have any leads."

Joy swallowed the lump in throat. She so badly wanted justice for Sabrina. It wouldn't change anything she'd been through, but it could keep a dangerous driver off the street and prevent them from hitting someone else. Plus, it would bring closure for Sabrina and all of them.

Rebekah turned to Bob. "Mr. Chorro, Ashley said you wanted to speak with me."

Bob nodded. "I've spoken with Sassie's attorney, Ms. Caltron. She's here to provide moral support—and legal advice if I need it."

Rebekah smiled. "I'm well acquainted with Ms. Caltron."

Cowboy Bob cleared his throat and glanced at Sassie, who crossed her arms. "I—" Bob stopped. Then he cleared his throat again. "I fled Charleston because I feared for my life," he said. "Sassie's grandfather was convinced I was a bad influence on Ernest and on Sassie too. Everything that happened to our group, he blamed on me." Bob glanced at Sassie and then stared at the floor as he clutched his cane. "I didn't realize what Ernest was doing until it was too late. I was afraid his associates might harm Sassie, and I was also afraid her grandfather would disown her because of me, because he blamed me."

"When did this happen?" Rebekah asked.

"Thirty-five years ago," Bob answered.

"And who exactly is Ernest and what was he doing back then?" Detective Osborne asked.

Sassie spoke up. "Ernest Crane is my first cousin. He served time for running a chop shop out of this building, over on the warehouse side. The money he accumulated was never found. Ernest said he'd earned the money honestly but that's not what the law said. Ernest blamed"—Sassie pointed to Bob—"him for taking it. Ernest said he put the money in the antique safe that was in this shop, thirty-five years ago, without me knowing it. I have no idea what the truth is. The safe disappeared the day before Ernest was arrested."

"Did you take the safe?" Detective Osborne asked Bob.

"Absolutely not. I admit I broke into the warehouse to see if it was still there, but I didn't steal anything. I've always known I was a suspect, along with Ernest. It broke my heart, but I decided to go far, far away from Charleston. But before I left, someone poisoned me."

"Who poisoned you?" Detective Osborne asked.

"I never found out," Bob said. "But I'm guessing it was someone in Sassie's family."

"What were you poisoned with?"

"Phenylenediamine."

Sassie gasped. Joy's heart began to race.

"What's that?" Detective Osborne asked.

Bob answered, "Hair dye."

"How was it administered?"

"Most likely in something I drank. I definitely ingested it."

"And you think it was someone in Sassie's family?" Detective Osborne asked. "And not Sassie?"

Bob nodded. "Of course the police thought it was Sassie. That was another reason I left. Without me around, they had less of a case."

Joy glanced at Sassie. She had a befuddled expression on her face.

"There's something else I need you all to know." Bob glanced at Ms. Caltron. "I haven't told this to anyone yet, but I'm fairly certain I'm right."

"What is it?" Detective Osborne asked.

Joy expected him to declare who he thought stole the safe on Friday and hit Sabrina.

"I believe I'm Ashley's father. She's the spitting image of my mother. I didn't know Sassie was pregnant when I left—I never would have gone if I'd known—but the math works. Ashley's my daughter."

"Mother." Ashley's eyes filled with tears.

Sassie's face grew red.

Joy wanted to ask Bob if he was Riley O'Connor, but before she could speak, he said, "Oh, wait." He looked at Rebekah. "I left out some important information. My name isn't Robert Chorro. It's Riley O'Connor. Hannah O'Connor Hollingsworth is my sister."

Joy sighed. She'd been right. Bob was Riley O'Connor.

Ashley groaned. "Mother, can't you ever tell the truth?"

Sassie took a step backward, into the hall.

Bob leaned on his cane and pushed himself up. "I'm sorry, Sassie. But I'm dying—I need to speak the truth. I need some closure, if that's possible." He turned back to Detective Osborne. "I didn't steal the safe, nor did I hurt Hannah. And I was in the hospital when Joy's daughter was hit. But I can bet that what happened last Friday is connected to what happened thirty-five years ago. There's no way it could all be a coincidence."

With that he slumped back down hard onto his chair and then slid to the floor. Everyone leaped to their feet, but Shirley reached him first.

Joy spent the rest of her evening marveling at Shirley's nursing skills. As Joy called 911, Shirley and Ashley attended to Bob. He was having difficulty breathing, and his pulse was weak. When the ambulance arrived, Shirley rode with him to the hospital.

It turned out that Bob's electrolytes were low. He agreed to be hospitalized overnight but said he'd leave again the next day. Shirley assured him no one would stop him.

At nine, between loads of laundry, Joy texted Sabrina, ANY BETTER?

BETTER. I'M REALLY HOPING I CAN GO HOME TOMORROW.

I HOPE SO TOO. SEE YOU IN THE MORNING.

Sabrina "loved" Joy's text, which warmed her heart. She didn't take it for granted that Sabrina had survived the hit-and-run and brain surgery—and was getting better. Joy had known tragedy. She knew no family was immune.

When she'd folded all of Sabrina's family's laundry and stacked it in the two baskets, she put her load in the dryer and then sat down at her laptop and did more research while it dried.

She googled *phenylenediamine poisoning*. It could cause gastritis, renal failure, vertigo, tremors, convulsions, and coma. She read more about the substance and then googled *Riley and Hannah O'Connor, South Carolina*. A few entries appeared for Hannah O'Connor Hollingsworth. Nothing appeared for Riley. Then she tried both names and *Georgia*. Nothing. Then *North Carolina*. A 1978 obituary popped up for Loretta O'Connor in Morning Star, North Carolina. Riley and Hannah O'Connor were listed as her children and an Emory S. O'Connor as her husband.

Joy googled Riley and Hannah's father. He passed away in 1981 in prison, three years before Riley and Hannah graduated high school.

Chapter Seventeen

Wednesday morning, as Joy stepped into Sabrina's room, a woman followed her. She was dressed in slacks and a blazer and said, "Joy Atkins?"

Joy turned to her. "Yes."

"I'm a process server here in Charleston. I have a subpoena from a court clerk in Harris County, Texas."

Joy's mouth dropped open. "Was it necessary for you to track me down in a hospital room?"

The woman extended a packet to Joy. "I was waiting for you near the gift shop but then followed you up here."

Joy shook her head in disbelief as she took the packet.

The woman said, "Have a good day," and headed back out the door.

"Mom," Sabrina said. "What's going on? Are you in some sort of trouble?"

"No," Joy answered, clutching the packet to her chest. "I wasn't going to tell you about this yet—and I don't think I should tell you unless you can promise me you won't worry about it."

"Mom—what is it? You're scaring me."

Joy sat back down. "Daybreak Oil and Gas has accused your father of embezzling money."

"What?"

Joy put the packet on her lap. "The subpoena is for our financial records."

"But how could he have done that?"

"They're saying he hacked into the system and it went undetected—until now," Joy explained. "They're claiming he embezzled money in 2012 and 2014—$500,000 from the company treasury is missing from each of those years—but I don't have hard copies of his investments from those two years."

"That's unlike Dad to have an incomplete set of records," Sabrina said. "He was so meticulous about that sort of thing."

"I know." Joy smiled, remembering his thoroughness. "I know he didn't embezzle any money. There's a mistake somewhere."

"Yes," Sabrina said. "I know Dad wouldn't do anything illegal." Her eyes filled with tears. "You've got to prove him innocent."

Joy opened up the packet. The deposition was for Friday, plus they wanted financial documents for the last seven years. She hadn't disposed of any records he'd kept, so she assumed she still had records through 2013. Still, two days away was too soon. "I'm going to contest this or at least try to get the date pushed back."

"Why?" Sabrina asked.

"Because you're ill. You're not even out of the hospital yet."

"I will be. This afternoon. I have another CT scan this morning—I'm going to pass it with flying colors."

Joy couldn't help but smile. "I bet you're right."

She left Sabrina's room a few minutes later, feeling as if the packet in her hand was a lit firecracker. Once she reached the gift shop, she left messages for both Carlos and Randi, explaining that she'd been subpoenaed and asking for their advice. Then she scanned the document and emailed it to Carlos.

She checked her phone repeatedly for responses from either of them over the next four hours, but neither called back.

At eleven, Lacy arrived, and just after that Evelyn stopped in. "Do you have a minute?" she asked.

"Yes," Joy answered, nodding to the back room. "How about a cup of coffee?"

"Thank you," Evelyn said. "Do you want one too?"

Joy stifled a yawn. "Please."

When they settled down at the table, Evelyn said, "I did some more research at the courthouse on Ernest Crane and found out that he challenged his grandfather's will last week."

"Didn't his grandfather die six years ago? Isn't it way too late to contest his will?"

"Yes, it seems so," Evelyn said. "But not too late to 'construe the will.'"

"What does that mean?"

"Challenge the wording of the document."

"Wouldn't that need to be done before probate?"

"Usually," Evelyn answered. "But it seems Ernest has come up with an addition to the will he claimed his grandfather mailed to him the second time he was in prison. Ernest is claiming he didn't know his grandfather had passed away until he returned to Charleston last week."

"Interesting," Joy said. Then, as Joy took her notebook from her purse, she told Evelyn what Bob Chorro, who was really Riley O'Connor, revealed the evening before.

"Riley O'Connor? He's Ashley's father?"

Joy nodded. "Well, that's what he said. And Sassie didn't deny it."

Evelyn shook her head. "That's quite the twist."

Joy agreed. "He's very ill, I'm afraid. That's why he's here. He said he wanted closure on his youth."

"Did he say anything about being poisoned back then?"

"Yes. You remembered correctly—he was in the hospital for three days."

"Who poisoned him?"

"He suspects someone in Sassie's family because the poisoning was phenylenediamine."

Evelyn gave Joy a questioning look. "I don't know what that is."

"It's an ingredient in hair dye."

"Hmm," Evelyn said. "And he doesn't suspect Sassie?"

"That's what Rebekah asked." Joy shrugged. "Bob—I mean Riley—still seems to be smitten with Sassie."

"I'm assuming he ingested the poison—it wasn't applied on his head?" Evelyn asked.

Joy shrugged. "Riley seems to think Ernest has the money that was in the safe. I got the impression he thinks it was Ernest who poisoned him too."

Evelyn wrapped her hands around her mug. "We don't know the lab results as far as Hannah, right?"

"That's right," Joy said.

"When will she find out?"

"Hopefully soon."

Did Ernest poison Hannah Hollingsworth to frame Sassie for the crime, hoping to increase his chances of getting the building? Did he poison Riley O'Connor all those years ago too? Or, was he trying to take Sassie down for testifying against him thirty-five years ago?

Long after Evelyn left the gift shop, Joy still hadn't heard back from Carlos or Randi. Finally, around one, her phone dinged.

She expected it to be one of them, but it was Sabrina. I'M BEING DISCHARGED. FINALLY! CAN YOU TAKE ME HOME? ROB WENT INTO THE OFFICE BECAUSE WE DIDN'T THINK IT WAS GOING TO HAPPEN.

YES, OF COURSE! Joy texted back. I'LL BE UP ASAP.

NO HURRY. IT WILL TAKE A WHILE.... I'M STILL WAITING TO TALK WITH THE DOCTOR.

Thankfully Lacy had come in at noon. Joy approached her and asked, "Any chance you can close?"

Lacy smiled. "Any chance Sabrina gets to go home today?"

"Yes." Joy beamed.

Lacy gave her a high five. "I can't tell you how happy I am to hear that. Although I know you're even happier than I am."

"Definitely," Joy said. "As long as Sabrina's brain is healed enough to go home. That's all that matters."

"They wouldn't send her home if not."

Joy agreed, but as she walked to the back room she took out her phone and sent Amanda a text. DO YOU THINK IT'S A GOOD IDEA FOR SABRINA TO GO HOME? AFTER THE SEIZURE YESTERDAY?

YES, Amanda responded. HER CT SCAN WAS CLEAR AND SHE'S ON MEDS. SHE'LL BE FINE. Joy was so relieved to have Amanda's knowledge and clear head to weigh in on Sabrina's health.

A half hour later, after Joy walked to her house to retrieve ingredients to make lasagna for dinner—Sabrina's favorite—and her car, she drove back to the hospital. By the time she reached Sabrina's room, Sabrina was trying to dress herself. She helped Sabrina get the T-shirt that Rob had brought for her to wear home over her wound.

"He didn't think to bring a button-up," Sabrina said.

Joy smiled. "This works." She stretched the neck of the T-shirt as she lowered it over Sabrina's head. "I haven't dressed you in thirty years."

"That's not true," Sabrina said. "You dressed me on my wedding day."

Joy laughed, remembering the seventy-five buttons up the back of Sabrina's dress. "That's right."

"Father's Day is Sunday," Sabrina said.

"Yes," Joy said, surprised at the jump in topic from Sabrina's wedding day to Father's Day. But on second thought, it made sense. Who had walked her down the aisle? Wilson, of course.

"Could you help me figure out dinner for Rob? Something simple but nice, to mark the day."

"Of course," Joy said. "I'd be glad to." She thought again of the large barbecues they used to have for Father's Day back in Houston. So much had changed with Wilson's passing. "I'll take care of dinner and make a peach cobbler." She used to make that dessert every June. It had been Wilson's favorite, and it was Rob's favorite too. The peaches were just starting to ripen. The timing was perfect.

The nurse came into the room, followed by Lance pushing a wheelchair. He grinned. "Ladies, I'm so happy I get to do the honors."

"We're so happy too," Joy said.

"Any word on the driver of the SUV that hit you?"

Sabrina shook her head. "I'm beginning to think there won't be."

"I'm determined to find out," Joy said. "We're not giving up hope."

"I'm with your mom," Lance said. "I'm convinced justice will prevail." He shivered. "I'm still having nightmares about you getting hit."

So was Joy, but she didn't say so.

The nurse took out Sabrina's IV and gave her a packet of discharge information. Then Joy left to get her car to meet Lance and Sabrina at the exit.

A half hour later, Joy had Sabrina in her house and resting on the family room sectional with the TV off and her phone put away, Mopsy out in the backyard, and the baskets of clean laundry on the dining room table. After she poured a glass of sweet tea for Sabrina, she began cleaning the kitchen. Her phone rang.

Carlos. Finally. "Hello," Joy said, stepping into the dining room and keeping her voice low. "I was afraid you weren't going to call me back." She continued on into the living room so Sabrina couldn't hear her.

"I was in court all day."

"Did you get my email?"

"Yes," Carlos said.

"Can you speak with the lawyer and court clerk and reschedule the deposition?"

"I don't recommend that," Carlos said.

"Why not?"

"An anonymous source for Daylight Oil and Gas has gone to the media. There are reports in the works."

"Reports accusing Wilson of embezzling money?"

"Yes," Carlos answered.

"How much are they saying he embezzled?"

"They think the original one million estimate might be the tip of the iceberg. Perhaps five million so far."

Joy laughed. "That's ludicrous. I don't have money like that."

"Have you found any evidence of other accounts where Wilson could have hidden money?"

"No. Absolutely not."

"Go through everything you have," Carlos said. "And buy a ticket for Friday morning, the first plane out of Charleston. That way we'll have time to talk before the deposition."

"No," Joy responded. "I need you to reschedule all of this for next week. I'm not leaving Sabrina this soon after brain surgery. Besides, they can't expect me to put together the documents in two days."

"It's a bad idea to reschedule the deposition. It makes you look as if you're hiding something. Yes, you legally have up to two weeks to gather documents, but you don't need that long. It's going to look like you need the time to get your story straight—not go through your files."

"I don't care what it looks like. Wilson is innocent. We can as easily prove them wrong next week as on Friday."

Carlos let out an audible sigh. "I'll see what I can do."

After Joy finished the kitchen and put the family's laundry away, the front door opened and Rob and the girls came bounding through. The rest of the afternoon and into the evening was spent making the lasagna, eating, doing dishes, playing with the girls, and getting them to bed.

As Rob read to Eloise and Mallory, Joy sat down on the sectional next to Sabrina. "What do you need before I go?"

"I need you to go to Houston on Friday."

"What do you know about Friday?"

Sabrina sighed. "Our walls are thin. There are no secrets in this house."

Joy grimaced. "I don't want you to worry. Carlos is going to try to get the deposition changed."

Sabrina shook her head. "I think you should go Friday. I'm doing fine. The girls will have their last day of sports camp. Rob is going to work from home tomorrow and Friday. I'll be fine, but Dad's reputation might not be, along with your finances."

Joy patted Sabrina's knee. She appreciated Sabrina's loyalty to her father and her concern about Joy's financial well-being.

"Who would frame Dad?" Sabrina's shoulders slumped a little. "Do you remember, after his funeral when we were back at the house, that someone mentioned that Dad left you a hefty retirement account?"

"I don't think so...."

"Something about how robust Dad's retirement accounts and his investments were."

"Whoever said it was probably assuming he had a good retirement," Joy said. "I think everyone who works there has substantial retirement accounts."

"I remember thinking it sounded weird," Sabrina said. "It was a man with short hair, wearing an expensive suit. Middle aged."

Joy smiled. "That describes most of the people Dad worked with." She had a vague memory of someone saying something. It had seemed odd, but she hadn't been offended. Honestly, not much—if anything—had offended her since Wilson passed away. It was as if she were immune to drama. Wilson had been taken from her much too soon—and yet the Lord had allowed it. Why should she be offended by what others did or said? Life was too precious to spend her energy, energy she could use to love others, on being offended.

She patted Sabrina's knee again. "I'll try to think of who said something."

Joy knew Wilson's reputation was important to Sabrina. Joy and Wilson had built a legacy together, one that benefitted Sabrina and her family. Joy wanted to honor that legacy, for all of them.

She thought of the legacy Sassie had built over the years, with the help of her grandfather. It was what she had to give to Ashley, yet Sassie's legacy seemed to be riddled with deceit.

Legacies had to be protected—with honesty and integrity.

"Could you help me to bed while Rob reads to the girls?" Sabrina asked.

"Of course." Joy stood and offered her hand to Sabrina.

A half hour later, Sabrina was asleep and the girls were quiet. Joy let the dog back in and then asked Rob, "What can I do to help tomorrow?"

"I don't know of anything. We have clean clothes and leftover lasagna. I believe we're all set."

"Call me if you think of anything," Joy said. "And I'll check in with Sabrina in the morning."

"Thank you for everything," Rob said. "I don't know what we'd do without you."

"Are you trying to flatter me?" Joy joked.

Rob chuckled. "No. Literally, I don't know what we'd do." His eyes grew moist.

Joy gave him a hug. "Well, the feeling is mutual. I don't know what I'd do without all of you. It's called being a family."

He hugged her back. "You must be exhausted."

"Not at all," Joy said. "Having Sabrina home is very invigorating."

Rob chuckled again. "I seem to be exhausted—and overwhelmed with relief."

By the time Joy arrived home, she was exhausted too, both physically and emotionally. Her surge of energy was all spent. She watered her outdoor plants and then intended to go through more of Wilson's records, but by the time she stood in front of his filing cabinet, she was so tired she felt ill.

She hoped Carlos could get the deposition rescheduled. If not, she'd have to go through the boxes tomorrow. She couldn't face another challenge today.

Chapter Eighteen

Thursday morning, as Joy sold a set of blue mugs with palmetto trees on them to a man from Florida, Hannah came into the gift shop. Joy gave her a wave and then listened to the man talk about his brother's open-heart surgery.

When the man left, Joy called out, "Hello!" to Hannah, who stood by the stuffed animals.

"Hi," Hannah answered as Joy walked toward her.

"How are you feeling?" Joy asked.

"All right. I just had more blood drawn to check my kidney function." Hannah fingered a stuffed pony. "How is Sabrina doing?"

"She went home yesterday, so she's much better, finally."

"That's good to hear. How are you?"

Joy smiled. "Much better too."

"I bet."

"I've been thinking about you," Joy said.

"After seeing me on Tuesday?"

"Well, I was thinking about you before and after that too. But, yes, that all seemed a little awkward."

"I'm sorry. I was feeling really out of sorts. Ashley and Sassie gave me a free pedicure and massage because they felt bad about what happened Friday, but then I got paranoid and wasn't gracious."

"I'm sorry," Joy said. "Did you get your toxicology results back yet?"

Hannah shook her head. "That's really weird. Those results were"—she made quotation marks with her hands—"'lost.'"

"That is strange."

"They're still looking. They seem to think they'll find them."

Joy wondered if Parker was pleased or frustrated with the missing results.

Hannah sighed. "It's been quite a week when it comes to medical conditions. Parker had his doctor's appointment yesterday morning."

"That's right," Joy said. "How did it go?"

Hannah held up her hands. "Who knows? He wouldn't let me go back into the exam room with him."

"Why not?"

"He said he was embarrassed about having a cognitive assessment."

"If he's having cognitive problems, shouldn't he have someone with him for the appointment? To remember what the doctor said?"

Hannah frowned. "That's what I said." Her phone dinged, and she glanced down. "Parker's on his way to pick me up—he dropped me off earlier. I've been trying to stay away from work, but he's insisting I come in today. Which means he's up to something."

"Any ideas?" Joy asked.

Hannah shook her head. "I just hope it doesn't have to do with the Crane Building. He's been obsessed with it for years. Not so much the building but the view of the harbor. He's been saying that the view is wasted on a salon and warehouse. He wants to raise the roof as much as the building committee will let him—you know, no buildings can be higher than the tallest church steeple in town, St. Matthew's."

Joy remembered Regina telling her that.

"He wants to develop the whole thing into condos. High-end condos. He's convinced he can build enough units on the property to make it all worth it."

Joy hoped her voice didn't give away her intense interest. "No affordable condos?"

"No," Hannah said. "He wants to make as much as possible. I'm pretty sure he met with Ashley last Thursday night to get her to convince Sassie to sell."

Joy raised her eyebrows.

Hannah lowered her voice. "Ashley's having financial problems." Hannah pulled her purse up higher on her shoulder. "I wanted to help Ashley, but Parker told me to stay out of it." She shrugged. "Sassie has never been very generous with Ashley. She made her take out student loans for college. Wouldn't give her start-up money for a business. That sort of thing."

"Has Sassie always been like that?"

"It's hard to know, right? I mean from middle school until we were in our twenties, she was pretty carefree," Hannah said. "But then Ernest got arrested, and Riley disappeared, and Sassie's granddaddy freaked out about everything, including Sassie being pregnant. She had to work really hard to re-earn her grandfather's trust, make her business successful, and raise Ashley on her own. She can be really focused on what needs to be done, in a really secretive way."

Hannah looked Joy in the eyes. "I think you know this and just aren't bringing it up."

"Know what?"

"That Riley is my brother—and also claims to be Ashley's father."

Joy didn't flinch. "I do know that."

"It's true. He's definitely Ashley's father," Hannah said. "I actually thought it might be a possibility this whole time. Riley and Sassie were secretive about their relationship because they didn't want her grandfather to know, but I suspected they were more than just friends. I felt betrayed that neither Riley nor Sassie were honest with me. But then I was so ashamed when it seemed Riley was involved in Ernest's criminal activity and then doubly so when he disappeared. Our mother died when we were little, and then our father went to prison when we were in high school, and Riley and I somehow managed to survive.

"I was so mortified when Riley became involved in Ernest's chop shop. I was sure he was destined to go to prison, just like our father. I tried to talk with Sassie about it once, about who Ashley's father was, but she said it wasn't anyone I knew, just a stupid mistake she'd made. She said she was happy to have the baby and never wanted to talk about it again. A couple of years after that I married Parker. Out of all of the men in our group, he turned out to be the only trustworthy one. Soon it was obvious we were having trouble getting pregnant, and it was hard to talk about babies at all, including about Ashley's origins. By the time I had Lindsay, Ashley was a teenager." Hannah's eyes grew misty. "Anyway, I had a lot of shame about my family, including—perhaps unfairly—about Riley."

"I'm sorry," Joy said.

"So am I. Not having Riley in my life all these years has been a big loss." Hannah frowned. "He has kidney cancer. He said it's hereditary." Tears sprang to her eyes. "That's what our mother died from."

"Oh." Joy reached for Hannah and Hannah accepted Joy's hug. "I'm glad you're getting your kidneys tested."

She sniffled. "This could all be a blessing in disguise."

"Hannah! Are you in here?" Parker came through the door of the gift shop. "Why aren't you answering your phone?"

Hannah spun around. "I'm talking to Joy—I didn't hear my phone."

Parker shook his head. "We need to go. We have a meeting in fifteen minutes." He turned around and headed back out the door. "I'm illegally parked."

"I don't know what's with him," Hannah said. "A midlife crisis? Early onset dementia? It's hard to tell. He has an appointment next week to go over his cognitive test. Hopefully he'll let me hear the results." She shook her head and then said, "Thank you for listening. It helps to talk."

"Thank you for talking," Joy said. "What you said helped me too."

Joy texted Sabrina to see how she was doing. Sabrina responded, Good, which filled Joy with relief.

Then in the early afternoon, Sabrina called. "You have to go to Houston tomorrow and do everything you can to clear Dad's name and protect your nest egg."

"I'm still hoping Carlos can delay it."

"No, Mom," Sabrina begged. "Go tomorrow. I'm fine."

Joy wanted to say, *Are you? What if you have another seizure?* Instead, she said, "I'll see what Carlos says."

"All right," Sabrina said. "But I don't want you *not* to go because of me."

At three o'clock, after Joy closed the shop, she called Carlos for an update.

"I couldn't get the date changed," Carlos said. "The attorney from Daybreak insists that we move forward as soon as possible. When do you fly in?"

"I haven't bought my ticket yet. I'll get a morning flight."

"Okay. You need to be here. The meeting is at two o'clock."

"All right," Joy said. "See you tomorrow."

"Did you find anything else in Wilson's records?"

"I haven't gone through all of them yet."

He stayed silent.

"I'm doing that tonight."

"All right," Carlos said. "The deposition is scheduled to take place in the third-floor conference room at the Daybreak building. Their attorney, the two of us, and a court reporter will be present. We can find a room beforehand to go over the records and I can answer any questions you have."

"See you then." Joy ended the call, feeling overwhelmed. The last thing she wanted to do was fly to Houston the next day. But she did need to clear Wilson's name.

When she reached home, she made herself a cup of mint tea and sat at her kitchen table, thinking about when she had picked up

Wilson's things from his office. Stephen Ford—whose cubicle was closest to Wilson's office—had greeted her. He seemed surprised to see her and said he didn't expect that she'd come so soon. Joy headed straight for Wilson's office, determined to get the task over as quickly as possible. Stephen said everything in the bookcases belonged to Wilson, but Wilson's assistant, Amy, clarified that everything in the *office* was Wilson's. She'd already taken all the office supplies and files that had to do with current projects.

Joy cleared the bookcases first and then the file cabinet, putting everything in cardboard boxes. When she arrived back home, she put the boxes in Wilson's office and left them there, intending to go through them later. With the information for each account included in Wilson's will, she worked with Randi to consolidate the accounts. She had no interest in keeping up with the market the way Wilson had.

A few months later, she had run into Amy at the mall, who said Stephen had been hired permanently as treasurer. Amy hadn't seemed too pleased when she said it.

When Joy decided to move, she finally went through the boxes and ended up giving all the photos to Sabrina, donating the books to the library, and marking the boxes from Wilson's office to go into the spare bedroom closet of the new house. When she came to Wilson's personal file cabinet in his office, she didn't bother to go through the documents. She just told the movers to load it onto the truck.

Joy finished the last drink of tea. She needed to check the file cabinet in the office. Perhaps the missing files were in it.

When Joy opened the top drawer of the file cabinet, she saw folders dated from 1985–2019 in the back. She pulled them out. They were photocopies of the papers she'd already seen. It made sense that Wilson had made copies, wanting a set both at home and his office. He was meticulous that way. She went through the files, year by year. There were no missing years—2012 and 2014 were included in the set Wilson kept at home.

She turned around to the box in the middle of the room from Wilson's office at Daybreak Oil and Gas. As she pulled the files out again, a sticky note fell to the floor. It wasn't in Wilson's handwriting. It read: *CHECK THIS AGAIN—REMOVE OR LEAVE? COMPARE TO 2014 ELECTRONIC STATEMENT.* Someone at work must have written it, but why would a note from someone else be in a personal file?

Joy thought of the box of cards from Wilson's memorial service, which were in a small plastic box on the shelf in the closet. After she retrieved it, she went through the envelopes, reading her name, over and over, on the envelopes. *Joy. Joy Atkins. Mrs. Atkins. Mrs. Wilson Atkins. Joy and family.*

She came to one that simply said: *JOY*. All in caps.

She opened the envelope and pulled out the card. It was signed, also all in capital letters, *STEPHEN AND DIANA FORD AND FAMILY*.

She went through the rest of the cards to see if there were any other "matches" but didn't find any. Stephen was the analyst who had worked for Wilson. He was the first to offer to go in on a Saturday if there were any problems. Wilson mentioned several times how much he relied on Stephen. Did he have access to Wilson's password and electronic files? Did he have access to Wilson's office when he wasn't there?

He was the one who met her when she went to the office to collect Wilson's things, who seemed unsettled that she'd come before he expected her. Had he meddled with Wilson's records? Had he broken into the system in 2012 and 2014 to make it appear that Wilson had embezzled money? Was it actually Stephen who'd done the embezzling?

She went through the bank records Wilson had saved, focusing on 2014. There were no odd deposits, certainly none for $500,000. Of course, Daybreak could claim Wilson had another account. If he did—and Joy knew he didn't—she didn't have access to it.

Joy glanced at the clock on her desk. Six thirty. It was five thirty in Houston. Carlos could still be in his office. She sent him a text. Do you have time to talk? When he didn't text back, she placed a call to him. He didn't pick up, so she left a voice mail.

Then she looked at tickets from Charleston to Houston for the next day. There were several seats both on the eight o'clock and ten o'clock flights. She booked the later flight.

Around seven, as she made herself a salad, Carlos finally called her back. She explained what she'd found—the copies of the missing files and the sticky note. "I'm certainly not an expert, but the note and the card seem to be the same handwriting. Perhaps Stephen found a way to access Wilson's computer and take some of his files."

"Scan everything and send the copies to me, and I'll forward them to Daybreak's attorney and the court clerk. But don't get your hopes up. Daybreak isn't going to cancel the deposition."

"All right," Joy said. "I have a ticket."

"Good. You're going to have to sit for the deposition no matter what."

After Joy ended the call with Carlos, she googled *Stephen Ford* on her phone and found a photo of him. She took a screenshot and texted it to Sabrina. DOES THIS MAN LOOK FAMILIAR?

Joy's phone rang immediately. Sabrina. Joy answered before it could ring a second time.

"That's the man who made the comment about Dad's retirement account," Sabrina said. "I'm sure of it. Who is he?"

"Stephen Ford. He was an analyst who worked for Dad and took the interim treasurer position, and then I heard that he got the permanent job too." She told Sabrina about finding the note written all in caps that matched the writing on the Fords' sympathy card.

"Weird. Be on the lookout if you see him tomorrow."

"I will," Joy said. "I've already sent Carlos everything I've found."

After her conversation with Sabrina, Joy continued researching Stephen Ford. He'd graduated from Duke in 2005 and worked for an oil company in North Dakota for five years. He started at Daybreak in 2010. She entered his name in a bankruptcy index search tool. His info popped up. He'd filed for bankruptcy in 2010. Joy stared at her screen. That certainly didn't mean that he'd embezzled the money, but it did mean he might have a motive.

She couldn't help but wonder if Wilson had known about the bankruptcy and what his response was. She vaguely remembered, years ago, Wilson talking about a young man in the office who'd lost a child to cancer and had battled with his health insurance company and lost. Could that have been Stephen?

Chapter Nineteen

Joy opened the gift shop the next morning. When Lacy arrived at eight, Joy retrieved her bag with the hard copies of the files and headed out to grab a taxi.

Two and a half hours later, she landed in Houston. After hailing another taxi, she arrived at the Daybreak building.

Carlos met her out front. "We have thirty minutes until the deposition. We can go to the conference room to talk."

Once they were settled at the table, Carlos said, "I've asked Mr. Marks if there have been any red flags concerning anyone else at Daybreak, if someone might be trying to frame Wilson." He paused.

"And?" Joy asked.

"He didn't answer me directly."

"Interesting," Joy said.

They went over Joy's documents again, including her accounts and bank records, going back to 2013. She told Carlos what she'd learned about Stephen's bankruptcy.

Carlos nodded. "I found that information too. After doing some more digging, I discovered it was over medical bills."

Joy felt sick to her stomach that Stephen and his family had gone through that. She knew Wilson would have been sympathetic too.

"I alerted Mr. Clark to our concerns."

The court reporter, who worked for a deposition service, arrived with Mr. Clark, the CEO of Daybreak. Stephen Ford, carrying a manila folder, followed them into the conference room.

Joy's eyebrows shot up, surprised he'd joined them.

"Hello, Joy." Stephen wore a designer suit and expensive shoes. "I'm so sorry to be seeing you under these circumstances."

Joy returned his greeting.

He turned to Mr. Clark. "I have those additional documents for you." On the outside of the folder was a neon sticky with a note written in all caps. *WILSON ATKINS: EMBEZZLEMENT CASE.*

As Stephen put the folder on the table in front of Mr. Clark, Joy took out her phone and took a photo of the sticky note.

Stephen looked at her, a puzzled expression on his face.

"I'm collecting evidence," Joy answered.

Stephen rubbed his brow. "You're the witness—not the investigator."

Joy shrugged and smiled sweetly.

"I can imagine you're upset," Stephen said. "And I'm sorry it's come to this. For the last year, I've defended Wilson, but the evidence seems conclusive. The investigation actually started right before Wilson passed away."

"Oh?" Joy hadn't heard that earlier.

Stephen looked away.

"Was Wilson questioned?" Joy asked.

Stephen's face reddened. "No. It hadn't gotten that far. But the missing money had been identified before he passed."

The court recorder finished setting up her equipment and said, "We need to get started."

Everyone took a seat except Stephen.

"Are you staying in the room for the deposition?" Joy asked him.

"No, ma'am," he answered.

"Please do," Mr. Clark said. "As the current treasurer of Daybreak Oil and Gas, we may have some questions for you too."

Stephen shrugged and said, "All right." He sat down at the end of the table.

Once the procedure began, Mr. Clark addressed Joy.

"I've gone through all of the documents you've submitted. Are there any other accounts you and your husband had that you know of?"

"No."

"Did he make any large deposits in any account that you're aware of in 2012 or 2014?"

"No."

"From what you sent, it appears there were two sets of the same records. One that Wilson stored in his office at Daybreak Oil and Gas and one he stored in his home office here in Houston, that were moved to your home in Charleston. Is that correct?"

"Yes." Joy glanced at Stephen. He was staring at the tabletop.

"Was there a difference in the two sets of records?"

Joy answered, "Yes. The records for 2012 and 2014 were missing from Wilson's office in this building but were included in the duplicate set in our home office. It appeared someone removed the files from Wilson's Daybreak office."

Mr. Clark shook his head. "That's speculation."

"The files are missing."

"Wilson could have removed them."

Joy took out the message written in all caps on the neon sticky note. "This fell out of the files from Wilson's Daybreak office."

Mr. Clark took it and glanced down the table at Stephen. Then he took a file from his briefcase. "Stephen, we started an internal investigation this morning after Mr. Martin forwarded additional information to me. We found several discrepancies in the retirement account transfers."

"Oh?" Stephen put his palms flat on the table.

"Our initial investigation showed that Wilson made the transfers. But when we dug deeper this morning, it seems someone else logged in during times when Wilson was out of the office. One time on vacation. Another time he'd traveled out to an oil rig to learn more about the business. He wouldn't have had access to the accounts either time."

Stephen shrugged. "I don't know anything about that."

"Are you sure?" Mr. Clark asked. "Because our internal investigation shows that whoever logged in did so from the computer in your office and somehow bypassed Wilson's password. It appears whoever did so figured out how to beat our system. IT is investigating that now to prevent it in the future."

Stephen turned his gaze to the tabletop and didn't respond.

The entire room was silent.

Finally, Mr. Clark asked Stephen, "Do you have anything to add to this discussion?"

Stephen stood. "Not until I speak with an attorney."

When the deposition ended, Carlos said he'd walk Joy to the exit.

"Thank you," she said. "First, I want to stop by the fourth floor and say hello to Amy, Wilson's assistant."

Mr. Clark overheard what she said. "Amy no longer works for Daybreak."

Joy's jaw dropped. "Since when?"

"Over a year ago. Stephen let her go and hired a new assistant."

"Oh."

"In fact," Mr. Clark said, "upon closer inspection I realized that Stephen replaced the majority of the department since he took over the treasurer position." He lowered his voice. "I'm grateful to you, Mrs. Atkins, for your work in responding to us. I'm guessing your motivation was to protect your husband's reputation and your finances, but it seems you may have shed light on where our true problem lies."

"I hope so," Joy said.

Mr. Clark smiled. "I'm relieved to find out there's another possible scenario. I couldn't reconcile that Wilson would have done anything like this, not the Wilson I know."

Joy sighed in relief. "Thank you."

When they reached the first floor, Carlos offered Joy a ride to the airport and she accepted. A half hour later, as they crawled through Friday afternoon traffic, Joy's phone dinged. It was a text from Anne. DO YOU HAVE TIME TO TALK? I HAVE SOME INFO ON ASHLEY.

Joy didn't want to talk about Ashley in front of Carlos. She texted Anne back. ON MY WAY TO THE AIRPORT TO RETURN HOME. I CAN CALL WHEN I GET THERE.

I need to pick up Addie. I'll just text you the info. It turns out Ashley lost her house two months ago. She and Barry were already behind on their mortgage, and the company foreclosed on her. It appears she lost everything when Barry died. His business was in the red by quite a lot, and he didn't have a life insurance policy.

Joy grimaced.

Ashley was thankful for Sassie's offer of the apartment and the job at the salon—but according to a mutual friend at church, Ashley is also extremely hurt that Sassie hasn't helped her out directly and chose to expand the salon instead of helping Ashley keep her house.

Thank you for the information, Joy texted back. The question is, How hurt is Ashley? Enough to collude with someone else to try to force Sassie to sell the building?

Who? Ernest? Riley?

I'm not sure, Joy responded. Maybe Parker. He was the one threatening to sue Sassie.

Interesting. Anne included a "thinking" emoji. Have a good flight back. TTYS.

Once Joy reached the airport and made it through security, she called Sabrina as she walked to the gate. After Joy gave her an update on the deposition, Sabrina said, "What a relief. Thank you so much for sticking up for Dad."

"I think the Daybreak CEO was having a hard time believing your dad would embezzle money. He was open to exploring other possibilities." Joy sat down away from any other travelers, in the far row of chairs at the gate. "Do you have time for a quick question?"

"Sure."

"Has Ashley spoken to you about financial problems? About her house being foreclosed on?"

"No. She hasn't said a word," Sabrina replied. "At one point she mentioned that she thought she'd rent the house out, that it was too big for her. When she moved into the apartment, I thought that's what she'd done. Why?"

"Don't say anything, but Anne heard that Ashley lost her house a couple of months ago."

"Oh no," Sabrina said. "I feel horrible about that."

"I don't think there's anything you could have done."

"I could have listened," Sabrina said.

"But only if Ashley had wanted to talk about it."

"That's true," Sabrina answered.

"I'll let you know when I get home," Joy said. "And then I'll come by in the morning."

"Great," Sabrina answered. "I'll look forward to it."

By the time the taxi from the Charleston airport dropped Joy off at her house, she felt exhausted. Had it really only been one day? Too tired to cook and feeling as if some exercise would do her good, Joy decided to walk up to the deli a block from the hospital and get a salad for dinner.

After she changed her clothes, she took off at a brisk pace. The sun was low in the sky as Joy neared the intersection of Harbor and Bay. A week ago, Sabrina had already been hit by the SUV.

"Joy!"

She turned toward the hospital.

Lance was jogging toward her. "How are you?"

Joy shaded her eyes. "Good. How are you?"

"Great! I just got off the phone with Detective Osborne."

Joy's heart raced. "Did she find out who hit Sabrina?"

"Not yet," Lance said. "But I remembered something. I'm pretty sure there was a sticker on the back bumper."

"Can you describe it?"

"Yes. BR."

"BR?"

"Yes. Those two letters."

"Interesting. What did Rebekah say?"

Lance shrugged. "'Thank you for the information.'"

Joy smiled, trying not to think about how many things "BR" could stand for. But Lance had done the right thing to report it. It wasn't exactly concrete evidence—a memory days old—but it could lead to something.

"I'll see you soon," he said. "Goodbye."

"Have a good evening." Joy continued on to the deli, passing by Sassie's salon on the other side of the street.

Once she had her salad, she decided to walk to the waterfront park and find a bench. There were still forty-five minutes of daylight left. She chose a seat south of the pineapple fountain and began eating her Greek salad as she looked out over the shimmering water of the bay.

As she took her last bite, she spotted a figure out of the corner of her eye. It was Ashley, darting behind a tree.

Joy stood. "Ashley! Is that you?"

Ashley stepped out from hiding, a sheepish expression on her face.

"Are you avoiding me?" Joy asked.

Ashley shrugged. "I'm just tired, is all." She stepped toward Joy. "How are you?"

"Confused," Joy answered. She patted the bench beside her. "Come sit with me."

Ashley complied.

Joy said, "I heard Parker met with you last Thursday evening."

Ashley nodded.

"What did he want?"

Ashley stayed quiet.

Finally, Joy said, "I'd really like to figure out who hit Sabrina and who took your mother's safe."

"I would too," Ashley answered. She hesitated and then said, "Look, it's no secret that Parker wants the Crane Building. Last Thursday he asked me to meet with him and then asked if it was up to me, if I'd sell him the building."

"What did you answer?"

"Probably. I still have a lot of debt from Barry's business. I'd rather not have to declare bankruptcy." She shuddered. "Mother could have easily bailed me out and saved my house, but she said no and then decided to expand the spa. That's been the story of my life. I've never been a priority to her." Ashley's eyes grew misty. "She insisted I call her 'Mother' because as a single mom she decided that sounded more respectful. Who does that? It's always seemed like I was an afterthought. And now I can see why she felt that way about me, after meeting Riley."

"I'm sorry," Joy said.

Ashley shrugged. "It doesn't matter. But what I don't understand is why Mother doesn't sell the building now. She's worked so hard. She should take it easy."

"Well," Joy said, "she's not that old. She doesn't seem like the kind of person who would want to *not* work."

"Parker's willing to pay Mother more than the building is worth. He said he'd rent her premium salon space in another building at a great price."

Joy could see why Sassie wanted to hang on to the Crane Building. It had been in her family for years. But she could also see why Ashley didn't feel supported by her mother—and why Sassie didn't want to bail Ashley out.

"Besides meeting with Parker about the Crane Building, did you speak with anyone else about it?"

"Like who?"

"Riley or Ernest."

"Absolutely not," Ashley answered. "I had no idea who either was until this week. I hope you believe me."

"I do," Joy answered.

"I should have said something about meeting with Parker," Ashley said. "I realize that."

Joy nodded. "That would have been helpful." She stood. "Are you heading home?"

Ashley shook her head. "Just out for a walk. How about you?"

"Headed home." Joy picked up her empty salad container from the bench. "Do you mind if I text you if I have any other questions?"

"Of course not." Ashley gave a little wave. "See you around."

As Joy walked, she thought of how easily Wilson's reputation was nearly ruined. Was someone trying to frame Sassie too? Could Ashley be involved? Or had Sassie staged a complex series of events to hide her years of deception? And if that was true, who had hit Sabrina? Someone Sassie had hired?

Joy shuddered. She didn't feel any closer to solving the mystery than she had a week ago.

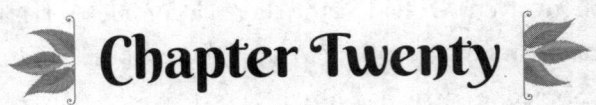

Chapter Twenty

ON SATURDAY MORNING, ROB WENT into his office to get caught up on a project while Joy made French toast for Eloise and Mallory. Then she and the girls took Mopsy on a walk. When they returned, Sabrina was awake and dressed. Her hair was swept over her wound, which had the dressing off now.

"I'll have Sassie trim it up before her grand opening." Sabrina wrapped her arms around her girls. "Rob is on his way home," she added. "You can go ahead and go—I know you have a date with Shirley and Regina."

Joy nodded. The three of them had pedicure appointments at Sassie's. Joy was looking forward to their "date." She was grateful Sabrina was well enough to be alone with the girls.

A block from the spa, Joy slowed as she saw someone with a cowboy hat sitting at a table outside a coffee shop. Was it Riley? The man sitting next to him looked like Ernest. Were the two in cahoots?

Joy found a parking space by the spa and then walked back to the coffee shop, but when she reached it, the two men were gone.

When she arrived at the spa, Shirley and Regina hadn't arrived yet. Joy checked in with Ashley and then headed up the hall, passing the pedicure area, and went straight to Sassie's office. The door was closed, so she knocked.

"Who is it?"

"Joy."

There was a pause and then Sassie said, "Come in."

Joy opened the door to find Sassie at her desk with a questioning look on her face. Joy stepped into the office and got right down to business—she knew Sassie was busy. "I think I just saw Riley at the coffee shop talking with someone who looks like Ernest."

"Riley is at my house, resting."

"Are you sure?" Joy asked.

"Positive. Did you speak with the men?"

Joy shook her head. "They were gone by the time I parked and went back."

Sassie locked eyes with Joy and then said, "Ernest comes around every once in a while to harass me. I ignore him. Maybe he had someone put on a cowboy hat so it would look like Riley, but I'm positive Riley wouldn't meet with him." She smiled. "Ashley said you and Shirley and Regina have pedi appointments today."

Joy smiled. "We do."

"I'm sending in complimentary chocolate strawberries, just because."

"Thank you," Joy said.

Sassie smiled again. "Have fun." Clearly she was done with the conversation.

Joy waved and stepped out the door, pulling it shut behind her.

When Joy reached the pedicure room, Shirley and Regina were already in their chairs. As Joy climbed into hers, one of the technicians brought in three plates of chocolate strawberries. "Compliments of Sassie," the technician said.

"Goodness," Regina said. "I've never had this happen before."

"Uh-huh," Shirley responded. "This is definitely a first." She shot Joy a questioning look.

Joy shrugged.

Shirley told the technician, "Please give Sassie a big thank-you. These look delicious."

After the pedicures were done, Shirley suggested they go out for lunch. "How about the Moonglow Café?"

"That sounds perfect," Joy said. Once they'd reached the café, settled at a window table, and ordered—crab cake sandwiches for Joy and Regina and a BLT salad for Shirley—the conversation fell to Sassie's Salon and Spa.

"I heard Riley O'Connor is back in town," Regina said.

"Who'd you hear that from?" Shirley asked her mother. Clearly Shirley hadn't said anything about Riley collapsing at the spa.

"I have my sources."

Joy and Shirley both laughed. That was one of Regina's favorite answers.

"Seriously, what do you remember about Riley O'Connor?" Joy asked.

Regina's eyebrows arched. "That he was poisoned," she said. "I took care of him when it happened." She'd worked at Mercy Hospital for years. "He was horribly ill."

"How long ago was that?" Shirley asked.

"Oh, thirty years or more."

Joy said, "Thirty-five to be exact."

"I don't think they ever figured out who did it. Most people thought it was Ernest Crane. But others thought it was Sassie."

Shirley stirred her straw around in her sweet tea. "Sounds like history repeats itself."

"Exactly," Joy said. "Unfortunately, a couple of mysteries were never solved back then—and we have three unsolved ones now."

"Mysteries," Regina said. "The Crane family has more than their fair share."

"What do you know about the Crane family?" Shirley asked.

Regina's dark eyes twinkled as she leaned forward. "I can't tell you what I had for breakfast, but I'll tell you what I know about the Crane family."

Joy took a drink of her tea, ready for some kind of revelation from Regina. She seemed to know what she was talking about—when it came to the past.

"Granddaddy Crane wasn't thrilled that Ernest and Sassie didn't go to college, and he was especially embarrassed that Sassie went to beauty school instead of going off to the university and joining a sorority. He was absolutely mortified when Ernest was arrested. Then for Sassie to have a child out of wedlock nearly broke him."

Regina continued. "But as Sassie built up her business, Granddaddy Crane grew proud of her. She devoted herself to her work, to her grandfather, and to Ashley. Her grandfather appreciated her so much by the time he died that he left the Crane Building and the family home to her. So Granddaddy Crane recovered from Sassie's indiscretions, but he never recovered from Ernest's first incarceration, nor his second."

"I wonder what might have happened if Mr. Crane had supported his grandson emotionally when he was released the first time," Shirley said. "You know, helped him get a job, housing, that sort of thing."

"Did you ever hear that someone besides Ernest might have poisoned Riley?" Joy asked.

"Oh, sure. Some said Sassie had done it. I wondered myself—it was rumored they'd been dating. Some said Sassie broke up with Riley. Others said the opposite." Regina shrugged. "I wondered if public opinion drifted to Ernest as the one who poisoned Riley once he was found guilty of running a chop shop." She took a sip of tea. "I never felt strongly one way or the other."

"Any chance it could have been someone besides Sassie or Ernest?"

"Sure," Regina answered. "But I have no idea who."

"What about the safe that went missing before Ernest was arrested the first time?" Joy asked. "Do you know anything about that?"

"Not really. I do know Sassie had an antique safe that belonged to her grandfather in her beauty salon. There were all sorts of rumors about what was inside. Gold coins. Confederate currency. Grandmother Crane's jewels. Sassie played up the safe, the same way she played up her trademark hair dye, otherwise known as Hannah's special formula. No wonder someone stole it."

Joy didn't have the heart to tell Regina the special formula was all a fabrication. She wondered if the safe holding treasure was a fabrication too.

"Later," Regina said, "it was rumored that Ernest's earnings from his chop shop were kept in the safe. But then, right before Ernest was arrested, the safe disappeared. Most people believed he'd hidden the money in it."

Regina patted her hair. "I was one of Sassie's first customers, I'll have you know."

Shirley smiled. "She should give you a longest-customer discount."

Regina laughed. "And an oldest-customer discount."

Joy laughed too—it was impossible not to when Regina found something funny. "What do you remember about Mr. Crane?"

"Oh, he was an old curmudgeon—but loveable," Regina said. "He had several properties around town that he rented out. As I said, he was disappointed that Sassie and Ernest didn't go to college, but I think he was proud of their business acumen, and he did eventually support that. At the time they opened their businesses, things were starting to turn around as far as the downtown economy—which is when the gentrification of Charleston began. And, although Ernest was in prison by then, Sassie's business miraculously wasn't damaged by Hurricane Hugo in '89." She took another sip of tea. "But back to Granddaddy Crane—I can't tell you how crazy he was about Ashley. He was her biggest fan. He'd come to their apartment after school and help her with her homework and fix her dinner while Sassie worked down in the shop."

As Joy listened to the conversation drift to another topic, she couldn't shake her suspicions. If it was true that Ernest hid the money in the safe, what did Sassie know about it, and when did she know it?

After Joy told Regina and Shirley goodbye, she headed back to the spa. She had more questions for Sassie. But Sassie wasn't there, and, although there were no clients in the lobby, Ashley was standoffish. And Joy couldn't blame her. She understood if Ashley was annoyed with her, but she hoped she hadn't ruined Sabrina's friendship with her.

"Mother is at home," Ashley said. "You could stop by if you want to." Clearly Ashley didn't object to Joy speaking with her mother. Most likely she just didn't want Joy asking her any more questions.

"Thank you," Joy said. "I'll do that."

When Joy arrived at Sassie's house, she parked and then decided to go to the front door.

Riley answered, without his cowboy hat on. His cheeks were even more hollow than they had been. But his smile was as big as ever. "Joy!" He held the door wide open and motioned for her to enter. "How are you?"

"Good. How are you?"

"Never better," he said. "Never better." He shut the door behind her. "But I'm guessing you're here to see Sassie, not me."

Joy said, "Well, it's great to see you but, yes, I do have some questions for her. However, first, I have a question for you."

"Oh?"

"Were you with Ernest outside of a coffee shop this morning?"

Riley looked sheepish. "Looks like you caught me."

"Why were you talking with Ernest?"

"He came by this morning after Sassie went to the salon. I couldn't ask him in—I knew Sassie wouldn't like that—so I rode with him to the coffee shop."

"Did he tell you he's making a claim for half of the Crane Building?"

Riley shrugged. "Come with me. Sassie's making crab bisque soup. Doesn't that sound delicious?"

She followed him into the kitchen.

"Oh hello, Joy." Sassie stood at the island, chopping an onion. "Ashley must have told you I'd come home."

"Yes," Joy answered. "I had some questions about the safe."

"Does it matter? Now that we all know Parker recruited her to try to convince me to sell?"

"We don't know for certain that Parker recruited her—we know he tried...." Joy's voice trailed off. "Remember, I want to know who hit Sabrina and if whoever took the safe is the culprit. I'm positive Ashley wants that too."

"Fair enough," Sassie said.

"Besides," Joy said, "I don't think you're guilty of any of the things you've been accused of—in the past or last Friday. I'd like to see you vindicated."

"Well, thank you." Sassie scraped the chopped onion into a pot on the stove. "But just to set the record right, I might not be guilty of anything illegal, but I'm guilty of doing plenty of harm."

"Sass," Riley said. "Please don't."

Sassie turned away from both Joy and Riley and stepped to the sink to wash her hands. Then she tore a paper towel off the spool, wiped under her eyes, threw the paper towel away, and then faced Joy, her eyes red. "What do you need to ask me?"

"I've been told the safe was in your salon before it disappeared the first time," Joy said. "Do you know what was in it then?"

Sassie shook her head and began chopping a celery stalk. "I never had a key to it. Granddaddy said it was empty. It was purely for decoration." She smiled. "Oh, there were plenty of rumors about what was in it. Pirate gold. Strings of pearls. My great-grandmother's jewelry." She kept chopping. "The women who came into my shop loved to speculate."

"When it disappeared, do you know if there was anything in it?"

"Do I know if Ernest stashed the supposed hundred thousand dollars he made from his chop shop in the safe? I absolutely have no idea. What I do know is that I didn't help him hide the money he made. Nor did I cooperate with the feds and get a plea deal so I didn't have to serve time. I don't know if Granddaddy or Ernest had the key, although I expect Ernest did. I never found a key in Granddaddy's things."

"Were you able to open it up the second time you found it?"

She shook her head. "I went through Granddaddy's things again, hoping to find a key. But I didn't find anything. I'd contacted a locksmith but didn't have an appointment yet."

"Anything else you can think of that would help me figure out who took the safe and hit Sabrina?"

Sassie shook her head. "Sorry."

"That's okay," Joy said. "I appreciate you talking with me."

"I'll walk you out," Riley offered. Once they reached the front door he stopped. "That meant a lot that you said you believed Sassie was innocent, both now and in the past. We were all so young when Ernest was investigated and then arrested. It caught us all by surprise, and we each reacted differently. Sassie closed down. I ran away. Parker and Hannah stayed here, ended up starting a relationship, and acted as if nothing ever happened. I don't think any of us realized back then what a turning point it was in all of our lives—but it was. I think we're all finally dealing with it, in our own ways."

That made sense to Joy.

"Some of us," Riley said, "just have more time to deal with it than others."

Joy patted Riley's arm. "You have an idea of how much time you have. Others have no inkling."

"That's true," he said. "We all have to do our best with the days we have, whether or not we know how many are left."

Chapter Twenty-One

On Sunday, Joy sat in church with Eloise on one side of her and Mallory on the other. Once the kids left for children's church, Joy tried to refocus her attention on the service. But her mind kept drifting to the events of the last week. Perhaps Ernest and Riley weren't in cahoots. Maybe Parker and Ernest were. Maybe they were working together to get the Crane Building from Sassie.

Perhaps Ernest had the key all along and was just waiting for the safe to be found.

Over and over, her thoughts kept going to Sassie and her group. Finally, as the pastor acknowledged the fathers in the congregation, she realized she'd been avoiding thinking about Father's Day. But she still had a father to celebrate—Rob—and she and the girls would do their best.

After lunch, she took her granddaughters to buy cards, a soccer dad chair, and ice cream to go with the cobbler she'd made that morning. Then she picked up the take-out order she'd placed the day before. She hadn't had time to barbecue for Rob, but she could still offer him brisket and ribs, along with greens, mac and cheese, coleslaw, and cornbread, all from the best barbecue place in town.

When they arrived at Sabrina and Rob's, the two were in the backyard, along with Hope, ready for the celebration. After they ate, as the girls played in the pool, Sabrina spoke quietly with Joy. "What's going on with Ashley?"

"Why do you ask?"

"She was texting me multiple times a day but stopped yesterday. When I texted her last evening, she never responded."

"I'm not sure," Joy said.

"Does it have to do with the missing safe? With everything that's going on with Sassie?"

Joy couldn't speculate what was going on with Ashley. A lot had happened in her own life during the last week.

"How about some of that cobbler?" Rob patted his stomach. "I need to keep working on my dad bod."

Joy and Hope laughed, and Sabrina shook her head but smiled. Joy headed to the kitchen to dish up the dessert, putting a scoop of ice cream on top of everyone's oversized piece of cobbler, inhaling the scent of the peaches and the hint of cinnamon as she did. There was nothing like peach cobbler in June to make it seem as if summer might, just this once, last forever.

After she and Hope, with the girls' help, finished cleaning up from lunch, Joy told her family goodbye. Sabrina needed to rest, and Rob planned to take the girls to the park to kick a soccer ball around. Hope said she wanted to get ready for the week, which Joy needed to do as well, but not yet.

Joy had more questions for Parker, and perhaps Hannah too. After his outbursts a week ago, Parker had been oddly quiet. It seemed he'd been busy with work, but why would he have been so accusatory of Sassie and then just stopped? Perhaps he'd sown the doubt he'd wanted to and watched it grow and spread like alligator weed. Perhaps that was his entire motivation.

Or perhaps he realized that drawing attention to himself was a bad idea.

Ashley might be guilty of talking with Parker and willing to conspire with him to get Sassie to sell the building, but Joy didn't think she was guilty of poisoning Hannah or stealing the safe. If she aided Parker in some way, Joy believed it was unwittingly.

Riley was either innocent or an award-winning actor. She couldn't rule out either Sassie or Parker. Hannah was close to both of them and believed both were innocent. Just like Sassie, she blamed Ernest for the breakup of their group, Riley's self-exile to Montana, and the stolen safe.

Joy considered texting Hannah about dropping by, but wasn't sure she should crash their Father's Day. She decided it would be even worse to just show up. She texted Hannah, asking if it would be all right if she stopped in.

Hannah texted back immediately to come on over, so Joy popped into Oceanside Bakery and bought a key lime pie. She was wise enough to know to sweeten the visit.

When she arrived at Hannah's, Sassie's car was in the driveway. Joy hesitated, fearing it might be awkward to speak with Parker and Hannah when Sassie was there. But she decided to go ahead and give Hannah the pie.

She walked up the steps to the front door and rang the bell. "Maybe it's him," someone called out.

"Mom, he wouldn't ring the bell."

A second later, Lindsay opened the door for Joy. "Hi," she said, a hint of confusion in her voice.

"Hello, Lindsay," Joy answered. "I brought a pie."

Now Lindsay looked confused also. "Okay."

"Your mom's expecting me. I was hoping to speak with her and your dad."

"Dad's not here. He had some sort of business thing to attend. But Mom's here. So is Auntie Sassie and Riley, who, it seems, is my uncle."

"Who is it?" Hannah called out.

"Joy—Ashley's friend."

That made Joy smile.

Hannah said, "I forgot to tell you she was coming. Invite her in."

Joy followed Lindsay up the stairs to the next level. The others were sitting around the table, which was covered with empty plates and platters. Joy held up the pie. "Ready for dessert? It's key lime."

"That was kind of you," Hannah said. "Lindsay made shrimp linguine for lunch, and we were planning to have ice cream for dessert. But key lime pie is much better."

"Great." Joy met Sassie's eyes and said, "Hi, Sassie. How are you?"

"Good," Sassie answered.

"How about you?" Joy asked Riley.

He smiled. "I can't complain."

"How's Sabrina?" Sassie asked.

"Much better, thank you." Joy glanced around. "Where's Ashley?"

"Sulking," Sassie said. "She's mad at me." She shrugged. "But what else is new?"

Riley had a pained expression on his face.

Lindsay took the pie from Joy. "Thank you." She put it on the kitchen counter and then cut it. Sassie stood and began clearing the table.

Hannah stood too. "Joy, do you mind if I ask you a question? In private."

"Sure," Joy said.

Hannah motioned to the staircase. "Let's go up to the office."

"Don't mind us," Sassie said, her voice sarcastic.

"Don't do that," Hannah said. "I'm trying to figure out what's going on with my husband. Joy's kept track of a lot of things that have happened this last week. I'm hoping she can help me."

"But you can't talk about it in front of us?" Sassie asked.

Hannah motioned to the kitchen, where Lindsay stood with her back to the rest of them.

Sassie shook her head with a "whatever" expression on her face. "This is all Ernest's doing. I don't understand why Detective Osborne doesn't arrest him. I don't know what you could possibly need to talk to Joy about."

Hannah ignored Sassie and continued up the steps with Joy following. When they reached the office, Hannah sat in a chair in front of the desk and motioned for Joy to sit in the other. "I thought of something that might be significant," she said. "Nearly every time

I go to the salon, Ashley fills my water bottle for me. Do you think she put something in it?"

"Did you see her put anything in it?"

"No," Hannah said. "And I didn't taste or smell anything unusual."

"There are a few poisons that are tasteless and odorless," Joy said. "Arsenic comes to mind. I imagine they tested for it."

Hannah shrugged. "Perhaps those results were lost with the others."

"Other poisons would be easier to hide in another drink besides water or in food."

"Like in a smoothie?"

"Perhaps," Joy said.

"Parker's been making me weight loss smoothies every morning for the last month."

"Weight loss?" Hannah didn't need to lose weight.

She sighed. "He's gotten on a health kick. He thinks we both should trim down."

"Oh." Joy found that unsettling.

"He said *we* but meant me," Hannah said. "He certainly doesn't need to drop any pounds."

Joy furrowed her brow. "Neither do you."

"Well, thank you, but compared to Parker I do." She sighed. "It's so hard to know what's going on with him. Does he have cognitive issues or is that a ruse? Is he going through a midlife crisis? How bad are our finances?"

"What do you mean?"

"It seems Parker made some unwise investments—or something." She shook her head. "I don't know. I work in the business, but I never know exactly what's going on. Really, I never have. He's so impulsive. I'm afraid he's done something really stupid—or he's going to." Hannah sighed. "All along I feared Riley had taken after our father and became a crook. I just let him go. I never tried to find him, never tracked him down. I assumed he was off somewhere, living a life of crime. But now it seems my brother was innocent of what I assumed he'd done all those years ago, and instead I married a man who isn't trustworthy."

"Is there anything specific that Parker has said or done that makes you think he's untrustworthy?"

Hannah winced and then lowered her voice even more. "He did say, two weeks ago, that he was tempted to 'make Sassie disappear' if she wouldn't sell him the Crane Building."

"Do you think he was serious?"

"Do I think he planned to kill her? No. Do I think he might be willing to ruin her business? Sadly, yes."

"Did anyone else hear him say he wanted to make Sassie disappear?"

"No," Hannah said. "But I have it on my phone."

Joy raised her eyebrows.

"We were up here, both working. The light fell across the waves late in the afternoon, and I got my phone and started recording it. Parker didn't know I was. He was crunching numbers and said, 'I need the Crane Building to make this all work. If Sassie won't sell it to me, then I'm willing to make her disappear.'"

"You have audio of that?"

Hannah took out her phone. Seconds later, Parker's voice came over the speaker, saying verbatim what Hannah had related.

"Why didn't you tell Detective Osborne about this?" Joy asked.

Hannah wrinkled her nose. "Parker was being so attentive, more than he'd been in months. He seemed so sure Sassie had a part in me collapsing."

"So what's changed?"

"The way he's been acting since then."

Joy leaned forward.

"Secretive," Hannah said. "Downright deceptive."

Joy looked around the office. "Have you searched the house? To see if there's anything suspicious?"

"Such as?"

"Poison?"

"I'll search after everyone leaves."

"Let's look now," Joy said.

"All right." Hannah motioned to the closet. "That's entirely Parker's. I don't go near it."

"Why not?"

"It's a mess. Have at it. I'll look through the desk drawers."

Joy opened the closet doors. She started at the bottom and worked her way up. There were binders for different projects, cables, a couple of monitors, and a laptop. Next were office supplies—printer paper, pens, and then a drawer with air duster cans. Joy peered behind the cans. Wedged in the back was a dark bottle. She grabbed a tissue from the table and picked up the bottle. It felt mostly full. She shook it. A little bit seemed to be missing. The label simply read $C_6H_4(NH_2)_2$. PHENYLENEDIAMINE. As Joy spun around to show Hannah, she heard someone coming up the stairs.

"Mom," Lindsay called out. "I have something to show you. It's in the basement. I've never seen it before."

"What is it?" Hannah asked.

"An old safe."

Joy and Hannah followed Sassie and Lindsay to a back room in the basement with a treadmill, an exercise bike, a weight machine, and a rowing machine in it. Riley arrived as Lindsay pulled the tarp off the safe, which was stashed in the closet. "I was looking for Dad's old laptop with photos from Father's Day when I was little," she said, wadding the tarp in her arms.

"That's Granddaddy's safe," Sassie said.

It was wrought iron and studded with hobnails. There was a name plate engraved with CRANE in the middle of the front panel.

"What now?" Hannah asked.

They all looked at Joy.

"I'll call Detective Osborne."

Joy placed the call. Rebekah didn't answer, so she left a message saying the safe was in Parker Hollingsworth's basement.

Riley, from where he sat on the weight bench said, "It seems probable that Parker is the one who stashed the safe down here."

"No," Sassie said. "Ernest did it."

Hannah pulled her phone from her back pocket. "I'll go through our security videos."

Joy's phone rang. Rebekah. Without returning Joy's hello, Rebekah said, "I'm on my way. Don't touch the safe."

Joy relayed the message to the group and then said, "Let's wait to see what Rebekah says before we decide what to do next."

Sassie crossed her arms. "I really don't think Parker took the safe. Ernest stole it, I'm sure of it."

"And stashed it here?" Joy asked.

"He could have," Sassie said. "He probably snuck it in here last Friday to frame Parker."

"There's no video of Ernest or anyone else bringing the safe here," Hannah said.

"How did the safe get in here then?" Sassie asked.

"Wait." Hannah stared at her phone. "The security system was turned off last Friday—all day long. Parker—"

"Or Ernest," Sassie said.

Hannah frowned at her. "—could have brought the safe here during that time."

"Would Ernest know how to turn the system off?" Joy asked.

"Definitely," Sassie said. "He's a thief."

Lindsay had slipped away and now returned with a tray loaded with dessert plates of key lime pie. "We might as well enjoy this as we wait," she said.

Fifteen minutes later, Rebekah called Joy, saying she was at the basement door. Lindsay hurried to let her in.

After they updated Rebekah about the phenylenediamine in Parker's office closet and Hannah's audio of Parker saying if Sassie wouldn't sell him the building he was willing to "make her disappear," Rebekah asked everyone to go upstairs while she dusted the safe for fingerprints. "I'll come up and let you know what I find."

Lindsay grabbed the tray of empty plates and led the way, followed by Hannah and Joy. Sassie and Riley were last. They all congregated in the living room and stared out the window at the incoming tide.

A few minutes later, Rebekah came up the stairs and stepped into the living room. "There are no prints on the safe. It's wiped clean."

"Now what?" Hannah asked.

No one answered her. They all stared at Rebekah, who exhaled slowly.

Joy spoke up. "What if Sassie contacts Parker and tells him she wants to talk about selling the building?"

"I will not sell the building." Sassie frowned at her.

"I know," Joy said, "but tell him you're willing to talk about it. You don't have to be willing to sell the building to do that. We need Parker to come home."

"That sounds like a good plan," Hannah said. "We'll confront him with the evidence and see how he responds."

Sassie didn't seem convinced. "Parker isn't the thief. Ernest is. He framed Parker."

"What about the threat he made about Sassie?" Riley asked.

"It wasn't a threat. It was Parker being Parker. Hyperbole. We've all heard him talk that way."

"Then let's get him here and prove him innocent," Rebekah said. "Then we can concentrate on Ernest."

"Perhaps the two were working together," Joy added.

"All right." Sassie texted Parker.

Immediately her phone dinged.

Sassie read the text silently and then read it out loud. "'Let's meet somewhere else. At the Crane Building.'"

Sassie said aloud, as she texted, "'I'm at your house. Meet me here.'"

Immediately the phone rang.

Sassie put it on speaker and held the phone flat in front of her face.

Parker, without saying hello, said, "Why are you at my house?"

"Because it's Father's Day. Remember Father's Day? Lindsay made you lunch."

"I had business I needed to take care of." Parker's voice grew louder and cheerier. "So you want to sell after all?"

"I want to *talk* about selling—see what you're willing to offer." Sassie glanced at Joy and then said, "We should talk now—before I change my mind."

Parker paused and then said, "All right. I'll be there in a half hour."

Once Sassie ended the call, Joy said, "We need to hide the cars and make a plan."

"Yes," Rebekah said. "First I'll call for backup, just in case."

Joy didn't care who the thief and hit-and-run driver was—if it was Parker or Ernest or somehow both—she just wanted the right person or persons held accountable.

Chapter Twenty-Two

When Parker arrived, Hannah met him at the door. "Where's Sassie?" he asked.

"She's here." Hannah started for the basement stairs.

"What she's doing down there?"

Hannah didn't answer him.

Parker didn't turn to see Lindsay, Joy, and Rebekah in the kitchen, nor Riley in the living room. He followed Hannah down the steps.

Lindsay followed her father. "Hey, Dad. Happy Father's Day."

"Thanks, Linds," he called back to her.

Joy and Rebekah started down next. When they reached the bottom, Hannah, Parker, and Lindsay were all in the workout room with Sassie. His voice carried. "You have to believe me, Sassie. I didn't take the safe. You know as well as I do it was Ernest. He must have stolen it and then broken into our house and hid it here. It fits his MO perfectly. He's trying to frame me."

"Have you seen Ernest?" Sassie asked.

"No, but I heard he's around. I'm so sorry I accused you of poisoning Hannah. It was clearly Ernest. He's up to his old tricks."

Sassie, with her hands on her hips, ignored Parker's declarations and said, "Do you have the key to the safe?"

"Why would I have the key?"

"Why would you have the safe if you don't have the key?"

"Ernest is the person you need to ask," Parker said. "This is all so déjà vu."

Sassie ignored him. "What was in the safe?"

Parker shrugged. "I have no idea."

"Ernest's hundred thousand dollars?"

Parker laughed. "You know Ernest hid all the money before he was arrested. That's why the safe went missing in the first place."

"We'll see," Sassie said.

Rebekah stepped into the room, followed by Joy, who heard footsteps and the thud of a cane coming down the stairs.

Parker turned as Riley entered the room. "What's going on?" Parker asked. "Who are you?"

Riley leaned heavily on his cane. "Parker, it's me. Riley."

Parker glanced at Hannah. She smiled.

He glanced around the room—at Joy and Rebekah and then at Riley again. "What are all of you doing here?"

Hannah answered, "Looking for the truth. Hoping to solve what happened to me, the safe, and Joy's daughter."

Parker rolled his eyes. "Well, I have nothing to do with the safe or Joy's daughter. And I certainly didn't poison you. Ernest did."

Hannah stepped closer. "How about you saying you wanted to make Sassie disappear?"

Parker groaned. "Hannah, I thought you were on my side."

Hannah held up her phone and played the clip.

Parker rolled his eyes. "Clearly I was joking."

Rebekah pulled the bottle from her satchel. "This was in your office closet."

He squinted. "What is it?"

"Phenylenediamine."

"I have no idea what that is."

"It's used in hair dye," Joy said. "It the substance that was used to poison Riley all those years ago."

"Wait." He spun around to Riley. "You really think I'm the one who poisoned you? I'm the one who carried you from the Crane Building to the hospital. I saved your life." He pointed to Hannah. "And I saved your life too."

"How did you save my life?"

"I convinced the doctors to run tests, told them I suspected you'd been poisoned. They wouldn't have discovered your kidney condition without me."

Joy shook her head. Parker put himself in the role of hero over and over.

"Parker," Rebekah said, "I've identified the vehicle that hit Sabrina. It's a black SUV with damage done to the grill, compatible with hitting a bike. It was rented, in your name, from Bay Rent-a-Vehicle."

"I don't know what you're talking about. I didn't rent an SUV, did I?" He turned to Hannah, shoving his hands in his pocket. "Did you tell her I've been having cognitive problems? That the doctor gave me a screening."

Hannah shook her head. "I don't have enough information to have an opinion about that."

"But you went to the doctor with me."

"You asked me to stay in the waiting room."

"I did?" He yanked his hands from his pockets, and a key clattered to the floor. Lindsay scurried and picked it up, holding it high.

"Is that to the safe?" Sassie asked.

Parker reached for the key and said, "Absolutely not."

Lindsay handed the key to Rebekah.

Everyone watched as Rebekah tried it in the safe. It worked. She swung the door open, but the safe was empty.

Hannah confronted Parker. "How long have you had that key?"

He pursed his lips.

"Thirty-five years?"

He didn't answer.

"Did you steal the safe thirty-five years ago too?"

"Absolutely not," Parker said.

"What about the money in the safe? You claimed your uncle gave you a hundred thousand dollars to start our business. Did you steal the money from Ernest?"

Parker laughed. "Did I steal the money Ernest stole in his chop-shop enterprise? That's rich."

Hannah shook her head. "That wasn't an answer."

Parker didn't respond.

Hannah continued. "Did you poison Riley thirty-five years ago? And poison me a week ago?"

Parker stayed quiet.

"Did you hit my daughter and flee the scene?" Joy asked.

Parker held up his phone. "I'm going to call my lawyer."

"Good idea," Rebekah said. "Tell him to meet us at the station." She stepped toward him. "You're under arrest."

Parker called his attorney and then left with Rebekah while everyone else trudged up the stairs to the living room. As the others sat down, Joy said, "I think it's time for me to go home."

"Please stay," Hannah said.

"I don't want to intrude. This should be a private time between old friends." Joy stepped toward the door. "I'll let myself out. I'll be in touch tomorrow."

Joy slipped out the front door. She knew what she needed to know. Parker had hit Sabrina and then fled the scene. And now he was under arrest.

As she started down the steps, she saw Ernest at the bottom. He peered up at her. "Hello, Joy. Is this Hannah's house?"

"Yes," Joy answered.

"Riley texted me the address and told me to come over."

Joy stepped to the edge of the stairs. "Come on up," she said. "This is definitely an evening for old friends to be together." The Dream Team, minus Parker, was back together at last.

As she reached her car, her phone rang. Roger. She accepted the call.

After saying their hellos, he said, "I wanted to check in to see how you're doing. Any chance you have time for dinner? If it hasn't been too long of a day already."

It had been a long day, but she answered, "I'd love to have dinner." It was an evening for new friends to be together too.

Monday, after Joy closed the gift shop, she sat down in the Grove with Anne, Evelyn, and Shirley to debrief.

"How are you holding up?" Shirley asked.

"Good," Joy answered as her phone rang. She placed her glass of sweet tea on the table and then said, "Excuse me just a second."

She pulled her phone from her purse and took a few steps away from the table. It was Rebekah.

"Joy speaking."

"I only have a minute," Rebekah said, "but I wanted to let you know that Parker confessed to hitting Sabrina."

Joy let out a sigh of relief.

Rebekah spoke quickly. "I'll be in touch soon—when I have more time to talk."

"I'm relieved," Joy said. "Have you called Sabrina?"

"Not yet. Do you want to tell her?"

Joy hesitated a moment and then said, "I think you should tell her. I'll stop by in a while and see how she's doing."

After she ended the call, Joy turned back to the table.

"Good news?" Anne asked.

Joy grinned. "Very good news."

"Hello!" Sassie started toward them, with Ashley at her side. "Joy, we've been looking for you. I was afraid you'd left already. Have you heard from Detective Osborne?"

"Yes." Joy motioned to the two chairs at the end of the table. As Sassie and Ashley sat down, Joy said, "Parker confessed to hitting Sabrina."

There was a collective sigh of relief around the table.

"He confessed to stealing the safe too," Sassie said.

"Did he say why he stole it?" Joy asked. "And why, after he did, he hid it in his basement instead of getting rid of it for good?"

Sassie leaned forward. "Yes. You know what a big talker Parker is. He answered all of those questions."

Joy raised her eyebrows. "And?"

"I'll start at the beginning. Thirty-five years ago, he stole Ernest's key to the safe and then the money Ernest had put inside," Sassie said. "Once he did that, he hid the safe behind a false wall in the warehouse. That was his first mistake. He should have just dumped it then, but he said he was afraid someone would see him if he took it out of my salon."

"Didn't he have to take it out of your shop and onto the street to get it to the warehouse?" Shirley asked.

Sassie shook her head. "There was a door that connected my shop and the warehouse back then. When the contractor found the safe and then Parker heard about it, he panicked. He knew I'd get the thing opened eventually and there wouldn't be any money inside. Parker figured I might begin to speculate what happened to the money and decided to steal the safe and drive up the Ashley River and dump it in a swamp. But once he hit Sabrina, he knew the police would be looking for a black SUV, so he took the safe to his house and hid it where he didn't think Hannah or Lindsay would look, planning to dump it later."

"Wow," Evelyn said. "I'm surprised the rental company didn't make the connection earlier."

"Parker bribed the guy at the rental company to write down that he'd returned the SUV two hours earlier so the time didn't match the crime and wasn't flagged," Sassie explained. "But then one of the workers who'd heard about the hit-and-run noticed the damage on the grill and contacted Rebekah."

"What about the other charges?" Joy asked. "Poisoning Hannah. Stealing the money from Ernest thirty-five years ago. Poisoning Riley."

"Detective Osborne said those investigations are continuing. She spoke to both Riley and Ernest this morning. I'm guessing they're looking into Parker's claim that his uncle loaned him money. According to Hannah, the uncle said he didn't. She called him this morning."

"Wow," Evelyn repeated.

Sassie let out a big breath and then said, "It seems Parker framed Ernest all those years ago. He was helping Ernest with his auto body business and had some men stealing cars for him, which he then sold for parts. He pocketed the money and got the men working for him to lie and testify that they were stealing for Ernest."

Evelyn's eyes widened. "So Ernest Crane went to prison for a crime he didn't commit?"

"Yes," Sassie said. "And lost the support of Granddaddy. And me. I've apologized to him profusely, both last night and today. Parker took so much from all of us, Ernest and Riley in particular."

"Has he confessed to poisoning Hannah? And poisoning Riley all those years ago?"

"Not yet," Sassie said. "But I imagine he will soon."

Joy focused on Ashley. "How are you doing?"

Her eyes were red-rimmed. "All right. It's a lot to process."

Sassie reached out and took Ashley's hand. "I've apologized to Ashley too. And to Riley for believing Parker's lies about him and not trying to find him and tell him he had a daughter." Sassie wiped a tear away. "I'm hoping that, with time, God will bring healing to all of us."

Sassie glanced around the table to Shirley, Anne, and then Evelyn. "Thank you, all of you," she said. "For helping Joy figure this out." Her gaze fell on Joy. "And my biggest thanks goes to you. I know your motivation was to find out who hit Sabrina, but your determination and perseverance solved so much more than that. After all these years we finally know the truth, thanks to you."

The next Saturday morning Joy and Sabrina drove to Sassie's Salon and Spa's grand reopening. Sassie had trimmed Sabrina's hair a few days before, adding volume to it so it easily hid her shaved area.

After Joy parked the car, the first thing she noticed was a new sign for the business. SASSIE & ASHLEY'S SALON AND SPA.

"Sassie took Ashley on as a partner." Sabrina clapped her hands.

"Isn't that great?" Joy beamed. Sassie had sent her a text the day before to tell her the plan.

As they neared the shop, Ernest held the door to the spa open for them. "Welcome," he said, with a wide grin on his face.

Joy introduced Sabrina, and Ernest shook her hand and said, "I'm so thankful you're all right."

"Thank you," Sabrina said. "And I'm glad you're back in town with your family, where you belong."

Ernest gave her a grateful nod and motioned for them to enter the spa. The new spacious lobby was for both the spa and the salon. Off the lobby was the manicure area and then the pedicure area, which were both open. The massage rooms were next. To the right was an open hallway to the salon. The entire salon and spa was now airy and modern—except that the business was still housed in a two-century-old building.

A crowd of people already filled the lobby. Hannah turned and waved. Lindsay, who carried a platter of chocolate strawberries, met Joy's gaze and smiled. Ashley came out from behind the U-shaped counter in the middle of the lobby and gave Sabrina a hug.

"I was hoping you'd be able to make it," she said.

Joy stepped to where she could see the pedicure area. All the chairs were filled. The person at the far end had a cowboy hat on.

"Is that Riley?" Joy asked.

"Yes," Ashley said with a laugh. "His goal is to get more men to get pedicures."

"That's a great idea," Joy said. "How is he feeling?"

"Better." Ashley exhaled. "Mother found a doctor for him here who is going to start a new treatment. We're hopeful."

Joy thought of all the families she'd prayed for in the gift shop building up to Father's Day. Now she said a silent prayer for Sassie, Riley, and Ashley, for their family.

Sassie, wearing a black dress, swept into the lobby from the salon. As soon as she saw Joy and Sabrina, she waved and hurried toward them. After she hugged Sabrina, she took Joy's hand and said, "Thank you. I feel optimistic again, like I did when I was young. Parker nearly cost me everything—and yet for all of those years I trusted him. Now, instead, because of you, what I lost thirty-five years ago has come back to me."

Joy looked at Ashley and smiled. "It was never truly gone."

"But it took the truth to bring it back," Ashley said, putting her arm around her mother. "We're all grateful for a new start."

As they talked, Hannah and Lindsay joined them. And then Ernest drifted over from the door and Riley soon drew closer too.

Joy felt their grief over Parker and his deceit and the years they'd lost, but she rejoiced in the reputations—and relationships—that had finally been restored.

Dear Reader,

In *Hair Today, Gone Tomorrow*, Joy becomes entangled in the lives of a hairdresser, Sassie Crane, and her group of friends from thirty-five years ago. Sassie owns a hair salon and spa and for years has provided stylish cuts and color, massages, manicures and pedicures—and extra care and attention to all of her clients. As a single mother, Sassie sacrificed and worked long hours to serve her clients and make her business one of the most respected in Charleston.

But when crimes from the past intertwine with crimes in the present, the fallout threatens Sassie's reputation. She faces losing everything.

At the same time, Joy's deceased husband is accused of embezzling a large amount of money from his place of business before he died. Joy and Sassie are women just past middle age with grown daughters, and they're both thinking about what sort of legacy their families will leave once they're gone. As Joy fights to protect her husband's reputation, she also fights to protect Sassie's, on the chance she's also innocent.

As a woman well past middle age myself, I've been thinking a lot about the legacy I'll leave too. And as a grandmother, like Joy, I feel more invested in the idea of legacy than I did before. Oftentimes we think of legacies as being property and money. But I, along with Joy, believe being a person of faith, a person of integrity, and a person who invests in the lives of others is the greatest legacy I can leave.

I hope you'll think about your own legacy and the legacies of those close to you as you read *Hair Today, Gone Tomorrow*.

Enjoy!

Signed,
Leslie

About the Author

LESLIE GOULD IS THE NUMBER-ONE bestselling and Christy Award–winning author of over forty novels. She and her husband, Peter, live in Portland, Oregon, and enjoy hiking, traveling, and hanging out with their adult children and baby grandson.

… The Story Behind the Story …

When my husband and I visited Charleston, we toured the core of the city by horse and carriage and also on foot, smitten by the architecture and gardens.

Early on, the city that was founded in 1670 had the reputation of being "Little London" with its European design and busy seaport. Later, in 1960, the Charleston Old and Historic District, which covers most of the historic peninsular heart of the city, was declared a National Historic Landmark. In 1966, it was added to the National Registry of Historic Places. Recently, for nine years in a row, *Travel & Leisure* voted Charleston the best city in America. Clearly this location is valued and cherished, and it has been through the centuries.

Because of the historic designations, the area's architecture has been preserved. St. Matthew's Lutheran Church is the tallest building in the city—255 feet to its steeple top. No building in the historic section of the city can be built higher, to preserve the integrity of the old city and the residential nature of downtown. (Regardless of the historic preservation status, because of the frequency of flooding and the waterlogged and sandy soil, it would be unwise to build skyscrapers in Charleston anyway.)

The combination of Charleston's reputation as a livable city and the scarcity of property to build on, has increased property costs in the area, a story that is familiar in many cities around the world.

At the heart of *Hair Today, Gone Tomorrow* is the Crane Building, which houses a hair salon and spa. Because of its location (near the waterfront) and its height (two more stories could be added), it's become a highly coveted and profitable property for some in the story, while it remains a sentimental property for others. So much can change over the course of a life of a person, let alone the life of a city—even one protected by historic designations. I enjoyed exploring those changes in *Hair Today, Gone Tomorrow*.

Good for What Ails You

South Carolina Peach Cobbler

Cobbler Ingredients:
- 1 stick butter
- 1 cup all-purpose flour
- 1 cup sugar
- ½ teaspoon salt
- 3 teaspoons baking powder
- 1 cup milk

Fruit Ingredients:
- 3 cups South Carolina peaches, peeled and sliced
- 1 cup sugar
- 1 cup water
- 1 tablespoon cinnamon (sprinkle on top before baking)

Directions:

Preheat oven to 350 degrees. Melt butter in large, shallow casserole dish. Mix together flour, salt, baking powder, and sugar until well blended. Add milk and stir. Pour mixture over melted butter. Do not stir. Combine peaches, sugar, and water in saucepan and bring to boil. Reduce heat and simmer for about 10 minutes. Spoon peaches on top of batter and pour liquid on top. Do not stir. Sprinkle cinnamon on top. Bake for 35 to 45 minutes. Let cool. Serve with vanilla ice cream.

Read on for a sneak peek of another exciting book in the Sweet Carolina Mysteries series!

Pain Relief
BY BETH ADAMS

ANNE MABRY LOVED DELIVERING FLOWERS to the maternity ward. She enjoyed the excitement that was always in the air, the tiny babies swaddled in blankets, the joy that permeated the whole floor. Each bouquet of flowers Anne delivered was a celebration that a new baby had just been born; a new life had entered the world, and the new little person's family and friends were rejoicing. Today she carried a gorgeous bouquet of pink lilies, which Anne was pretty sure had been grown in her friend Joy's own garden. Joy was a master gardener and often brought in flowers she'd grown herself in her backyard garden to include in the bouquets sold here. The lilies gave off the most heavenly scent, and they would brighten any hospital room.

This bouquet of flowers was to be delivered to… Anne checked the card again. Room 321. Toward the end, then. She smiled as she walked the hallway, and she waved at her friend Shirley Bashore as she passed the nurses' station. She edged to the side as another nurse wheeled a bassinet past her, and then she ducked to the other side of the hallway as Luke Merritt, a member of the transport team, pushed two empty wheelchairs toward the elevators. A woman was taking pictures of a couple posing with a newborn just ahead. She nodded at two doctors, chatting as they walked past in white coats. She smiled at a woman—a new grandmother, Anne guessed—holding a tiny squalling infant carefully in her arms as she wandered back and forth outside the rooms. Finally, Anne made it to room 321, and she knocked gently on the partially closed door.

"Come in," someone called from inside. Anne pushed on the door gently and held out the flowers as she walked in. "Celeste Wright?" Anne smiled at the woman sitting up in the bed.

"Yes." Her long dark hair was disheveled, and the dark half moons under her eyes betrayed her exhaustion, but the woman still looked blissfully, radiantly happy as she held a nursing infant against her. A man lay on the couch by the windows, shirt rumpled, glasses askew, a bewildered smile on his face.

"Special delivery," Anne said. She set the vase down on the console by the bed. "Congratulations." It always seemed impossible that newborn babies were really this small. This one had a full head of dark hair and that cone-shaped head that often signaled that the birth had been difficult. It would return to its normal shape shortly. "Your baby is beautiful."

"Thank you. She is gorgeous, isn't she?" Celeste nodded at the flowers. "Who are they from? Do you mind checking?"

"Not at all. You've got your hands full." Anne leaned in to read the little white note attached to the stems. "We're so happy for you and can't wait to meet Caroline Lily. Love, Momma and Daddy."

Anne smiled. "Aw, lilies for Caroline Lily."

"That's nice," Celeste said. She looked down at the baby. "Did you hear that, little peanut? Your grandparents can't wait to meet you."

"Is there anything you need?" Anne asked, moving toward the door.

"No, we're good," Celeste said.

Anne slipped out of the room, leaving the new parents to attend to their baby. Those first few days were overwhelming and exhausting and wonderful all at once. She walked back down the hallway, cringing when she heard a woman cry out in pain. Labor was miserable, but it was so worth it. Anne passed a number of rooms, and the small waiting area for families, and the bathrooms. She waved at Olga Dotov, a member of the custodial staff, pushing her cart away from the recovery room. And up ahead—wait.

Anne couldn't have seen that right. She backed up and looked into the open doorway of the C-section recovery room. Was that...?

Anne stepped inside. The room was empty. It was often empty, as it was only used by patients who had just had a caesarean birth, and they didn't perform too many of those here at Mercy Hospital. But there at the end, just in the sight line of the doorway, was a medication machine. Anne didn't know all the details about how it worked, but she knew that when a doctor prescribed something for a patient, a nurse was able to log in and enter their credentials, and the drawers on the machine would slide open so the item could be retrieved and given out. It was roughly the size of the industrial copier they'd used in the St. Michael's church office, but instead of compartments for paper, this was filled with drugs. She knew that the drawers were meant to be closed, except when a nurse was taking medication out. It was supposed to be a very secure way to dispense and track prescriptions. So why were several of the drawers standing open right now, when no one was in the room?

She stepped closer. Three...no, four of the machine's drawers were open, and two of them had shards of plastic broken off at the top, as if...well, Anne wasn't even sure what. She peered inside the first drawer, and instead of the rotating carousel that dispensed the right medication, she saw mangled plastic, as well as a bunch of small white pills. What in the world...? Anne straightened up and saw that the screen showed a blinking red Error!

Someone had broken into it and taken medication. But how? And who? And which ones were gone? Anne wasn't sure, but she realized she had to tell someone—right away. She turned and hurried out of the room and back down the hall to the nurses' station. Shirley was still there, thank goodness, typing something on one of the computers lining the long desk.

"Shirley!" Anne said. "The machine! Someone broke into it."

"What?" Shirley looked up, her eyes narrowed. Another nurse sitting next to her—Anne thought her name was Gina—looked up too. "Which machine?"

"The medicine one," Anne said. "With drawers?"

"The Pyxis?" Shirley looked over at Gina, who was already pushing her chair back.

"Yes. That one. In the C-section recovery room."

"Show us," Shirley said, standing. Anne nodded and started off, Shirley and Gina following just a step behind. Anne hurried to the recovery room, and when they got to the doorway, Shirley gasped. She rushed forward to examine the broken machine.

"Oh my goodness," Gina said softly. She crouched over the open drawers.

"It looks like someone jimmied them somehow," Anne said.

"It does indeed," Shirley said. "And it appears…" She let her voice trail off.

"Demerol?" Gina suggested. "That's usually in this one." She tapped the drawer closest to her. "And oxycodone."

"This one is hydromorphone and hydrocodone," Shirley said, shaking her head.

"Fentanyl," Gina added.

The names sounded familiar to Anne. "Are those drugs for… pain?"

"Those are all powerful opioids," Shirley confirmed. "And they've been cleaned out. Someone broke into this machine and took a huge amount of dangerous opioid medications."

The next fifteen minutes were a blur, as hospital administration was called in and Shirley and Gina blocked off the recovery room. "In case whoever did this left fingerprints," Shirley explained. Anne knew it was also important to make sure no one accessed the medication that remained in the open drawers. Whatever it was, it could be dangerous if taken in the wrong circumstances.

"Tell me what you saw," Garrison Baker asked Anne again as several members of the hospital administration swarmed around the machine. Anne had already told Paige, the charge nurse on shift today, but she repeated the story, such as it was.

"Did you see anyone in the area?" he asked when she finished.

"There were people all around," Anne said. "It's always busy here."

Anne repeated her story to the police a few minutes after that, first to Officer Escobar and after that, to Detective Albert Lee.

"What time did you find the machine open?" Detective Lee asked. The police had set up a temporary command station in an unused delivery room, and he was seated on a swivel stool by the computer. Anne sat awkwardly on the bed, as if she were being examined—and it felt like she was.

"I didn't check my watch, but I would guess it was around twelve thirty or so. I had just come back from my lunch break when Aurora assigned me to deliver flowers."

"When was the last time you were in that recovery room?"

"It's been months. Maybe years. I don't really go into the rooms like that, where they're dealing with patients just out of surgery. I'm not a medical professional or anything, just a volunteer."

"Is there more than one door to the recovery room?"

"I believe there's just the one that goes to the hallway, but you may need to ask a doctor or nurse to be sure."

"Who else was in the area at the time?"

"There were so many people all around," Anne said.

"Tell me the names of anyone you remember seeing." Detective Lee took notes in a little black notebook, and he peered up at Anne through thick-framed glasses. Anne had worked with him before, and he was a nice guy. If he came across as a bit intense... well, she supposed this was an intense situation.

"Okay." Anne thought back. "Well, I saw Olga right before I noticed the drawers were open. She was right outside the recovery room."

"What's her role?"

"She's on custodial."

"She cleans the rooms?"

"And empties the trash. Strips and remakes beds. That kind of thing."

"When you saw her, had she come from inside the room with the machine?"

"I don't know. It's possible, but I didn't see." Anne wanted to be careful to speak accurately, given the stakes here.

"Who else?"

"Well, I had just come from delivering flowers to a woman down in 321. Celeste. But she was in bed holding her baby."

"We'll be interviewing all of the patients on the floor to see if they saw anything," Detective Lee said. "For now, let's focus on anyone you saw in the hallway or near the room with the machine."

"Okay. Um, I remember there was a baby being wheeled to the nursery. I don't know the name of the nurse who was pushing the bassinet, but it wouldn't be hard to find out."

"We'll figure out who that was." Detective Lee made a note in his notebook.

"I saw Shirley and a few of the other nurses when I passed the nurses' station," Anne continued. "Gina was there the first time. And Kitty as well. But there were probably other nurses out on the floor, tending to patients."

"We'll interview everyone who was on duty. Anyone else?"

Anne closed her eyes and thought. "Wait. There was the transport. Luke Merritt. I saw him pushing a couple of wheelchairs."

"A transport is…"

"An employee who moves things," Anne said. "They bring patients and equipment from place to place throughout the hospital."

"Got it. Does Luke work on this floor usually?"

"He works all over the hospital," Anne said. "They all do."

"Anyone else?"

"Not that I can think of specifically. But like I said, there were a lot of people around."

He nodded, scribbling something on the page. "When did you go into the recovery room?"

"When I saw that the drawers were open."

"How long were you in the room?"

"I don't know. Maybe a minute? Probably less. I just saw that something looked odd and went to go check it out. As soon as I realized what was wrong, I went and told Shirley."

"How quickly would you say you moved, once you realized something was wrong?"

"As quickly as I could." Why was he looking at her like that? "I don't think it took me thirty seconds, if that." He didn't really believe…

"Remind me of what your duties at the hospital are?"

"I'm a volunteer, so I do whatever Aurora, the volunteer coordinator, assigns me to do. Often it's delivering flowers, like today. Sometimes I do patient discharge, or I fill in at the front desk. Whatever needs to be done."

"So you roam around the hospital at will?"

"Not at will. Like I said, I do whatever task I'm assigned. But I do get to see many different parts of the hospital, yes."

"Do you ever have access to the Pyx—" He glanced down at his notes. "The Pyxis machines?"

"No. You have to have a log-in to use the system. It checks your fingerprint and everything. Only people who need to access the medications can. I don't have anything to do with dispensing medicine, so I can't."

"But you know what the machines do and where they are and roughly how to use them?"

Anne hesitated. He couldn't sincerely think she had anything to do with this, could he? "I have probably seen most of them, but I honestly couldn't tell you where they are. I don't really pay attention to them, since, like I said, I can't access the medication. And I'm unsure how they work, beyond the basics."

"Why don't you tell me what you know?"

Anne nodded. "I believe that when a doctor prescribes a medication for a patient, the pharmacy department enters that into the server that runs all the connected machines. As soon as it's in the system, a nurse can log in and enter the patient number, and the Pyxis machine's drawer will pop open so they can take the drug out and administer it to the patient. The machines are restocked by the pharmacy regularly."

"They're like vending machines but for extremely powerful and addictive medication?" Detective Lee's head was cocked.

"In some cases," Anne admitted. "I don't think all the medicine in them is addictive. I don't really know."

"So you don't know what medicine is stored in the machine?"

"I assume it's the basics. Whatever is needed. I've never really thought about it. Gina and Shirley said that the medicine that was taken today was all opioids."

He scribbled on his notepad as she spoke.

"Do you have any idea who might have wanted to get into the machine?"

"No. If they were right that opioids were taken, and I suppose there are plenty of people who might want to get to those." Anne stuffed down the twinge of dread she felt. "I know those are easily abused."

"Do you know if any of the people you saw on the floor today might have reason to want to get their hands on opioids?"

Anne wasn't sure what to say. Did she think any of the people she'd seen in the hospital this afternoon abused opioids? "I really wouldn't know," she said. "I hope not."

"Have you ever used opioids?"

"What?" She shook her head. "I mean, after a gallbladder surgery many years ago, they gave me a prescription for Vicodin, but I didn't end up using them all. Not since then."

He eyed her. "Can you think of anything else you'd like to tell me about what you saw today?"

Anne couldn't tell what he wanted her to say. He seemed to think she could have done it, or else knew who did. If she was aware of who had broken into the machine, didn't he think she would say so?

"If I remember anything else, I'll be sure to let you know," Anne said.

Detective Lee looked down at his pages of notes and nodded. "Right. I have your contact information. I'll give you a call if I have any more questions. Don't leave the area, please."

"Like, the area of the hospital?"

"Charleston. Just in case we need to talk to you again."

He thought she might leave town? Was he for real? Did he honestly think she could be responsible?

A Note from the Editors

WE HOPE YOU ENJOYED ANOTHER exciting volume in the Sweet Carolina Mysteries series, published by Guideposts. For over seventy-five years, Guideposts, a nonprofit organization, has been driven by a vision of a world filled with hope. We aspire to be the voice of a trusted friend, a friend who makes you feel more hopeful and connected.

By making a purchase from Guideposts, you join our community in touching millions of lives, inspiring them to believe that all things are possible through faith, hope, and prayer. Your continued support allows us to provide uplifting resources to those in need. Whether through our online communities, websites, apps, or publications, we strive to inspire our audiences, bring them together, and comfort, uplift, entertain, and guide them.

To learn more, please go to guideposts.org.

Find more inspiring stories in these best-loved Guideposts fiction series!

Mysteries of Lancaster County
Follow the Classen sisters as they unravel clues and uncover hidden secrets in Mysteries of Lancaster County. As you get to know these women and their friends, you'll see how God brings each of them together for a fresh start in life.

Secrets of Wayfarers Inn
Retired schoolteachers find themselves owners of an old warehouse-turned-inn that is filled with hidden passages, buried secrets, and stunning surprises that will set them on a course to puzzling mysteries from the Underground Railroad.

Tearoom Mysteries Series
Mix one stately Victorian home, a charming lakeside town in Maine, and two adventurous cousins with a passion for tea and hospitality. Add a large scoop of intriguing mystery, and sprinkle generously with faith, family, and friends, and you have the recipe for Tearoom Mysteries.

Ordinary Women of the Bible
Richly imagined stories—based on facts from the Bible—have all the plot twists and suspense of a great mystery, while bringing you fascinating insights on what it was like to be a woman living in the ancient world.

To learn more about these books, visit Guideposts.org/Shop